Cambridge Essentials

Science

Jean Martin Andy Cooke
Sam Ellis

Extension 8

 CAMBRIDGE
UNIVERSITY PRESS

CAMBRIDGE UNIVERSITY PRESS
Cambridge, New York, Melbourne, Madrid, Cape Town, Singapore,
São Paulo, Delhi

Cambridge University Press
The Edinburgh Building, Cambridge CB2 8RU, UK

www.cambridge.org
Information on this title: www.cambridge.org/9780521725705

First published 2008

Book printed in the United Kingdom at the University Press, Cambridge

A catalogue record for this publication is available from the British Library

ISBN 978-0-521-72570-5 paperback with CD-ROM

Contents

Take advantage of the CD

Cambridge Essentials Science comes with a CD in the back. This contains the entire book as an interactive PDF file, which you can read on your computer using free Adobe Reader software from Adobe (www.adobe.com/products/acrobat/readstep2.html). As well as the material you can see in the book, the PDF file gives you extras when you click on the buttons you will see on most pages; see the inside front cover for a brief explanation of these.

To use the CD, simply insert it into the CD or DVD drive of your computer. You will be prompted to install the contents of the CD to your hard drive. Installing will make it easier to use the PDF file, because the installer creates an icon on your desktop that launches the PDF directly. However, it will run just as well straight from the CD.

If you want to install the contents of the disc onto your hard disc yourself, this is easily done. Just open the disc contents in your file manager (for Apple Macs, double click on the CD icon on your desktop; for Windows, open My Computer and double click on your CD drive icon), select all the files and folders and copy them wherever you want.

Take advantage of the web

Cambridge Essentials Science lets you go directly from your book to web-based activities on our website, including animations, exercises, investigations and quizzes. Access is free to all users of the book.

There are three kinds of activity, each linked to from a different place within each unit.

- **Scientific enquiry:** these buttons appear at the start and end of each unit. The activities in this section allow you to develop skills related to scientific enquiry, including experiments that would be hard to carry out in the classroom.

- **Check your progress:** these buttons come half-way through each unit. They let you check how well you have understood the unit so far.

- **Review your work:** these buttons come at the end of each unit. They let you show that you have understood the unit, or let you find areas where you need more work.

The *Teacher Material* CD-ROM for *Cambridge Essentials Science* contains enhanced interactive PDFs. As well as all the features of the pupil PDF, teachers have links to the *Essentials Science* Planner – a new website with a full lesson planning tool, including worksheets, practicals, assessment materials, guidance and example lesson plans. The e-learning materials are fully integrated, letting you see the animations in context and alongside all the other materials.

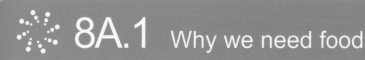
8A.1 Why we need food

You should already know | Outcomes | Keywords

Why we need food

We need food to survive. A healthy person who stops eating lives for about 40 days.

Food gives us the raw materials that our bodies use…

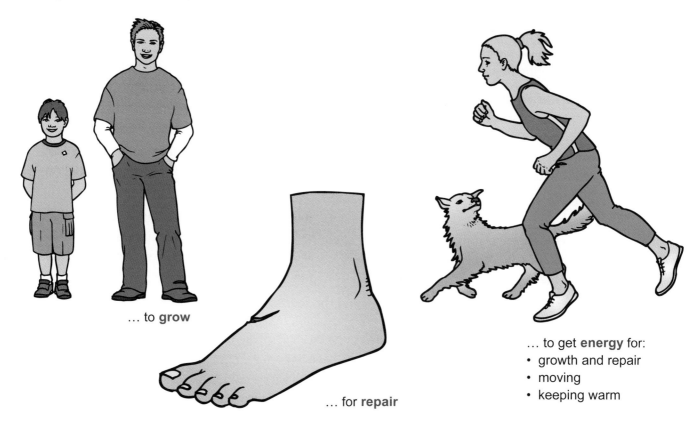

… to **grow**

… for **repair**

… to get **energy** for:
• growth and repair
• moving
• keeping warm

Question 1

We call the food substances that our cells use **nutrients**. They include:

• **proteins** for making new cells;
• **carbohydrates** and **fats** for energy;
• small amounts of **vitamins** and **minerals**.

Question 2

We are what we eat

Proteins are the main raw materials for making new cells. So proteins are particularly important at times when we are growing quickly.

Question 3

Protein foods.

Taribo has a normal diet.

Ntege has kwashiorkor. Kwashiorkor is a disease caused by a lack of proteins in his diet.

Question 4 **5** **6**

When we cut ourselves, some cells are damaged, some die and others are lost when we bleed. Our bodies have to make more cells to repair the wound and to replace the lost and damaged cells. Cells in our bodies are continually dying and being replaced by new ones. For example, a red blood cell lasts for only about four months. New red blood cells are made all the time to replace the ones that are worn out.

Look at the photographs. The wound gradually healed up. Eventually, there was no sign of it.

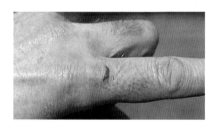

George's finger after an accident.

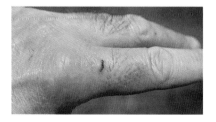

George's finger is healing up.

Question 7 **8**

| You should already know | Outcomes | Keywords |

We need energy for:

- growth and repair of cells;
- moving;
- keeping warm.

We release most of this energy from the **carbohydrates** and **fats** in our food.

starchy

sugary

Carbohydrate foods.

  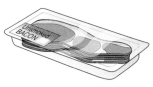 

Fatty foods.

| Question 1 | 2 | 3 |

Muscles contract to make us move. To contract, muscles need energy. So, the more we move around, the more energy we need.

We measure the energy used in kilojoules (kJ).
Look at the table.

Activity	kJ per hour
sitting	63
standing	84
walking	750
swimming	1800
walking upstairs	4184
sprinting	5183

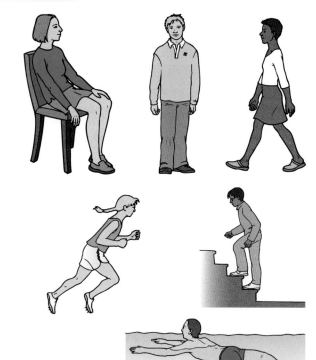

| Question 4 | 5 | 6 | 7 |

Mini but mighty

We need small amounts of **vitamins** and **minerals**. Although the amounts are very small, they are very important for our health.

In the 1740s, up to two-thirds of sailors on long voyages died of a disease called scurvy. When they were away from land for a long time, they didn't eat any fresh fruit or vegetables. So they didn't have any vitamin C in their diet. Lack of vitamin C causes scurvy.

Minerals such as calcium and iron are also important. Calcium is a raw material for making bones and teeth, and we need iron for making red blood cells.

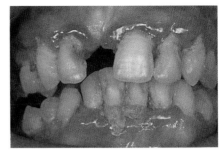

Scurvy causes bleeding gums as well as more serious symptoms.

The label shows some of the nutritional information from a packet of Sugary Puffs cereal.

Water and fibre

Most foods contain a lot of **water**. If you have eaten a water melon, you will know how watery food can be. Even your body is two-thirds water.

Fruit and vegetables contain a lot of **fibre**. Fibre is the cellulose of plant cell walls. Our bodies cannot break it down, so it goes right through the digestive system. But it gives the muscles of the digestive system something to push against, helping to move food along more easily. Without it, you'd be very constipated! In fact, fibre and water make up a large part of the bulk of your food.

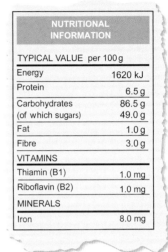

NUTRITIONAL INFORMATION	
TYPICAL VALUE per 100 g	
Energy	1620 kJ
Protein	6.5 g
Carbohydrates	86.5 g
(of which sugars)	49.0 g
Fat	1.0 g
Fibre	3.0 g
VITAMINS	
Thiamin (B1)	1.0 mg
Riboflavin (B2)	1.0 mg
MINERALS	
Iron	8.0 mg

fish

vitamins A, D

egg

vitamins B, D

milk

vitamins A, D; calcium

liver
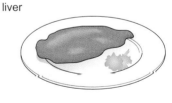
vitamins A, D; iron

vegetables
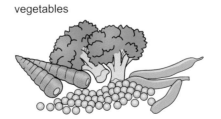
vitamins A, B, C

wholemeal bread

B vitamins, iron, calcium

Question 14

Foods containing vitamins and minerals.

You should already know   Outcomes   Keywords

Water in your diet

Water is an important part of your diet. You don't just get it in drinks. There is a lot of it in food, more in some foods than others.

Having enough water in the body, or being <u>hydrated</u>, helps to keep your body working properly. It reduces the risk of headaches and heatstroke (in hot conditions). There is also some evidence that it improves learning.

Question 1   2

Drinking water improves test results

This is the claim made following experiments at an Edinburgh primary school. Test results improved when pupils could have a drink of water at any time in the school day.

One theory is that water helps nerve impulses to pass. So being hydrated makes children better able to learn.

Finding out how much water is in food

Mrs Tasker asked her class for ideas. She set her class some preliminary work using books to research a way of finding out how much of various foods is water.

No one found that actual information but Bryan found an experiment about the amount of water in soil. Using the same idea, he suggested an experiment:

- Find the mass of the food.
- Heat it to get rid of all the water.
- Cool and find its mass again.
- The loss in mass will be equal to the mass of water that was in the food.

Anna found out that you needed to repeat the heating and cooling several times until two masses were the same. This is called <u>heating to constant mass</u>. You do it so that you can be sure that all the water has gone.

Lisa suggested chopping the food to increase the surface area and dry it faster.

We could heat the food.

We need to heat to constant mass.

We could chop the food up first.

Question 3

Mrs Tasker was pleased with the ideas so far. But she pointed out that they hadn't described how to heat the food.

Working out the best way to heat the food

Mrs Tasker suggested that the class needed to do some **preliminary tests**.

They decided to try out their ideas using apple to find out which one worked best.

	Heat over Bunsen flame		Dry on an open shelf at 20 °C		Heat in an oven at 100 °C		Heat in an oven at 300 °C	
Size of apple pieces	cut into eight	chopped up small	cut into eight	chopped up small	cut into eight	chopped up small	cut into eight	chopped up small
Mass at start (g)	140.8	136.4	142.3	143.5	138.6	136.7	133.6	139.1
Mass after 40 mins (g)	12.7	10.1	137.6	135.2	103.5	100.8	10.9	10.1
Mass after 1 day (g)	not done	not done	69.1	67.7	17.3	16.2	9.4	8.4
Mass after 7 days (g)	not done	not done	28.5	28.9	17.3	16.2	not done	not done
Loss in mass (g)	128.1	126.3	113.8	114.6	121.3	120.5	124.2	130.7
% loss in mass	91	92.5	80	80	87.5	88	93	94
Observations	black (burnt)	black (burnt)	brown mouldy	brown mouldy	brown	brown	black (burnt)	black (burnt)

Results of preliminary test.

Planning the investigation

The pupils looked at the data. Then they planned their investigation.

Question 4 / 5 / 6 / 7

The pupils decided that the best plan was to:

- chop up the food;
- find the mass of the food on a digital balance;
- heat in an oven at 100 °C;
- heat to constant mass.

They also discussed how to make sure that they got reliable results.

For results to be reliable, they must collect enough data and it must be accurate.

Question 8 / 9

You should already know

Outcomes

Keywords

What is a healthy diet?

A balanced, healthy diet contains the correct amount of each food group. We can get a balanced diet in all sorts of ways. Many people in richer countries like the USA and the UK get much of their **protein** from meat. Most people in poorer countries like India and China rely more on eating cereals and beans for their protein.

Question 1 2 3

Here is an analysis of the main nutrient, water and **fibre** contents of four foods.

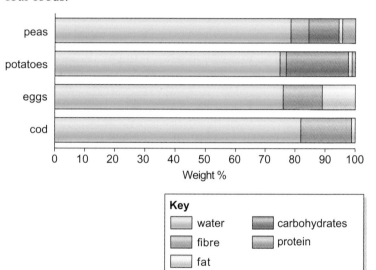

Key
- water
- fibre
- fat
- carbohydrates
- protein

A West Indian meal of rice, prawns and vegetables.

A Chinese meal of noodles, prawns and vegetables.

Question 4 5 6

A healthy, balanced diet is different for different people.
The things that affect how much of each food group you need include:

- your age;
- whether you are male or female;
- your body size;
- the activities and job you do.

For example, a person doing heavy building work needs more **fats** and **carbohydrates** for energy than a person sitting behind a desk all day.

A European meal of meat, potato and vegetables.

Question 7 8

Check your progress

When the nutrients in your food pass into your blood, we say that you **absorb** them.

Modelling what happens in your digestive system

In science, we sometimes use **models** to help us understand how things work. Look at the diagram. We can use this model of the gut to find out which substances can pass into the blood and which can't.

Question 1 2 3 ────────────────

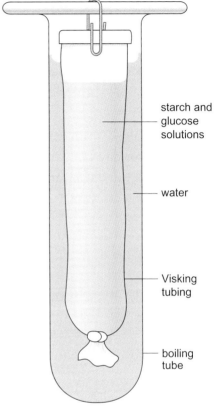

starch and glucose solutions

water

Visking tubing

boiling tube

What actually happens

Look at the diagram. Only the particles of vitamins, minerals and some sugars such as glucose are small enough to be absorbed.

You cannot absorb the large, insoluble molecules of fats, proteins and some carbohydrates. You have to break them down into smaller molecules. We call this process **digestion**. It happens in your digestive system.

After digestion, the small molecules pass into your blood and are transported to your cells.

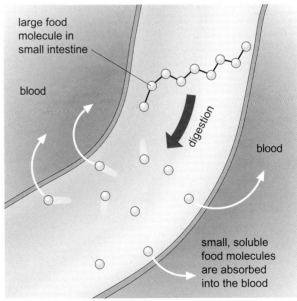

large food molecule in small intestine

blood

digestion

blood

small, soluble food molecules are absorbed into the blood

Absorption in the small intestine.

Question 4 5 ────────────────

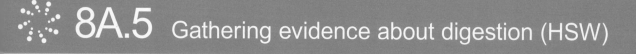
You should already know   Outcomes   Keywords

Your digestive system

Your food travels 8 to 9 metres through your digestive system from your mouth to your anus. The journey takes between 24 and 48 hours.

If food goes through too quickly, it is not broken down into the nutrients that you can **absorb**. If the surface area of your digestive system is not large enough, you will not be able to absorb all the nutrients.

Question 1

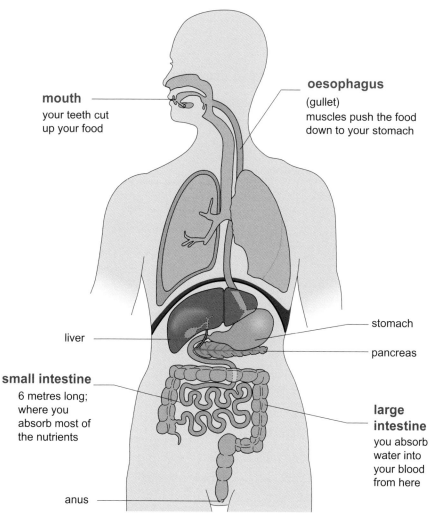

mouth
your teeth cut up your food

oesophagus
(gullet)
muscles push the food down to your stomach

liver

small intestine
6 metres long; where you absorb most of the nutrients

stomach

pancreas

large intestine
you absorb water into your blood from here

anus

Over 300 years ago, the ancient Greeks described many of the organs of the digestive system. They found out by dissecting dead bodies. It was harder to find out what each part did.

More ways of investigating

In the 1760s, an Italian priest called Lazzaro Spallanzani did experiments on his own body to find out about the digestion of food. He swallowed wooden blocks with holes containing meat and collected them when they passed out of his anus. He discovered that the food in the wooden blocks had disappeared. Spallanzani also made himself vomit and showed that the liquid vomit dissolved away meat. Sometimes he swallowed food on a piece of thread and pulled the food out before it was fully digested.

Question 2

Lazzaro Spallanzani.

What enzymes do

We now know that Spallanzani's meat disappeared because **enzymes** had broken it down. We know that cells in some parts of our digestive systems release these chemicals and that they break down large molecules of food into smaller ones.

Question 3

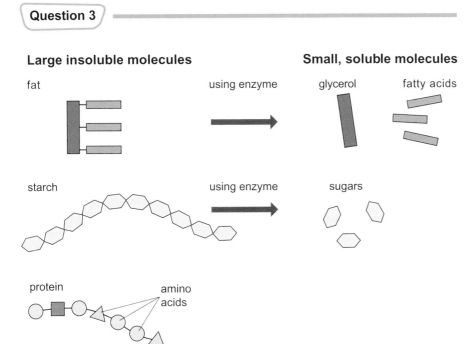

Large insoluble molecules   **Small, soluble molecules**

fat   using enzyme   glycerol   fatty acids

starch   using enzyme   sugars

protein   amino acids

We now know what is produced when different foods break down.

Question 4

Scientists continue to research what happens in the digestive system. They have found out that:

- different enzymes break down different foods;
- different enzymes work best in different conditions – for example, some work best in acidic conditions, others in alkaline.

Often doctors and specialist scientists work together to find out more about illnesses. Look at the photographs.

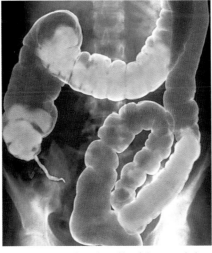

The patient drank a liquid containing a harmless barium compound. This is an X-ray taken when the barium reached the large intestine.

Doctors can use a tiny camera on the tip of an endoscope to photograph inside the digestive system.

Question 5 **6** **7**

You should already know

Outcomes

Keywords

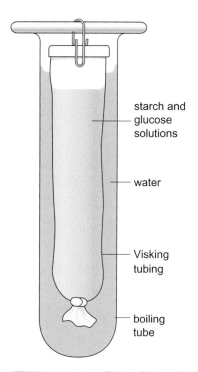

- starch and glucose solutions
- water
- Visking tubing
- boiling tube

Remember the model gut

The starch molecules are too large to pass through the tubing into the water. They are also too large to pass through your **small intestine** lining. So you have to break them down. Then they can pass through the lining into your bloodstream.

Your small intestine is adapted for **absorption**. It is long. It has a thin lining, a large surface area and lots of blood capillaries to carry away the nutrients.

Question 1 2 3 4

Every cell of the body needs nutrients. Cells need them for growth, repair and as an energy source. So the bloodstream carries the nutrients absorbed in the small intestine to all parts of the body. They are carried in solution in the blood plasma – the liquid part of blood.

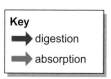

Key
→ digestion
→ absorption

vitamins and minerals

intestine lining

sugars

blood vessels in intensive wall

amino acids

fatty acids and glycerol

starch

proteins

fats

Question 5 6

What happens to the nutrients

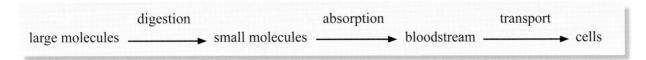

digestion   absorption   transport

large molecules ⟶ small molecules ⟶ bloodstream ⟶ cells

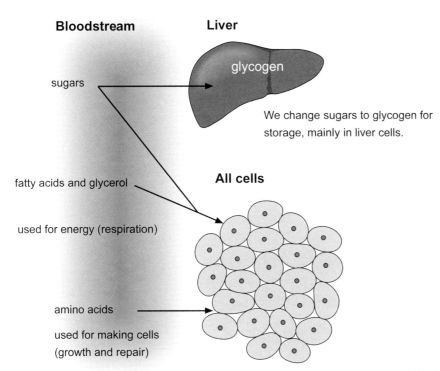

Bloodstream   **Liver**

sugars

glycogen

We change sugars to glycogen for storage, mainly in liver cells.

fatty acids and glycerol

All cells

used for energy (respiration)

amino acids

used for making cells (growth and repair)

What happens to the products of digestion.

Question 7 **8**

What happens to the waste

All the undigested food, including **fibre**, is got rid of in **faeces**.

We say that we **egest** it. Faeces are mainly fibre, water and bacteria.

Review your work

Summary ➡

8A.1

1 Look at the pictures.
Write down:

  a <u>two</u> reasons you need to make new cells;

  b <u>three</u> uses for energy in your body.

2 Find out a use in your body for:

  a <u>one</u> vitamin;

  b <u>one</u> mineral.

3 On average, a pregnant woman needs 76 g of protein per day.
A woman who is not pregnant needs less.

  a Explain why a pregnant woman needs extra protein.

  b Find out how much protein a woman normally needs.

4 Write down <u>two</u> differences between the children in the photographs.

5 Write down <u>two</u> foods that will improve Ntege's health if he can get them.

6 Some children don't eat enough protein foods. Will this have any long-term effects on them? Explain your answer.

7 Explain what is happening to make the wound on George's finger heal up.

8 Wounds take longer to heal if the person doesn't eat enough protein foods.
Why is this?

8A.2

1 Write down <u>four</u> energy foods that you eat.

2 Children's growth can be slow when they don't get enough energy foods.
Suggest why.

3 Nathan is 24 years old. He is no longer growing.
What will happen to him if he doesn't get enough energy foods?

4 When we are sitting still, what do our bodies use energy for?

5 Between which <u>two</u> activities in the table does a person getting dressed fit?
Explain your answer.

6 Adam is a distance runner. On the day before a race, he eats lots of carbohydrate foods.
Suggest why he needs to do this.

continued

7 Why do we need more energy when standing up than when sitting down?

8 Look at the photograph.
Describe some effects of scurvy.

9 Write down <u>one</u> food that contains:

   a vitamin C;

   b vitamins A and D, and the mineral iron;

   c calcium.

10 What is the main nutrient in Sugary Puffs?

11 Which mineral is found in Sugary Puffs?

12 Write down <u>one</u> vitamin in Sugary Puffs.

13 Find out the effects of a lack of <u>each</u> of the two B vitamins.

14 Explain why you need water and fibre in your diet.

8A.HSW

1 Look at the newspaper article.
What evidence is there of a link between hydration and learning?

2 In your group, discuss what you would do to investigate the effects of drinking enough water on learning.

3 Look at the speech bubbles. All three ideas are a useful part of the experiment plan.
Explain why <u>each</u> idea is useful.

4 What <u>two</u> kinds of preliminary work did the class do before they planned their investigation?

5 The pupils rejected heating over a Bunsen burner and in an oven at 300 °C because the apple lost more than just water.

   a What evidence is there that more than just water was lost?

   b Suggest what else was lost.

6 Suggest <u>two</u> problems of drying the apple at 20 °C.

7 These tests didn't show whether chopping up the apple made a difference to the time taken to dry the apple.
What extra tests can the class do to find out the answer?

8 Look at the pupils' plan.
Suggest reasons for each step.

9 In your group, discuss other ideas for making:

   a the investigation safe;

   b the results reliable.

8A.3

1   In the West Indian meal, the rice is the main energy source.
    What provides most of the protein?

2   In the Chinese dish, the prawns provide most of the protein.
    What is the main energy source?

3   Which part of the European meal contains most of the proteins
    and fat?

4   Which of the foods on the graph contains the most:

    a   water?

    b   protein?

5   What is the main nutrient in potatoes?

6   Which nutrients in the graph are missing from cod?

7   Suggest what the following people need to eat.

    a   Mmapula, a 13-year-old girl living in South Africa.

    b   Steve, a professional footballer in the UK.

8   Janet is breastfeeding her baby.
    Find out what she should eat and drink.

8A.4

1   Which part of the model represents the blood?

2   What does the Visking tubing represent?

3   Later, there is glucose in the water around the Visking tubing
    but no starch.
    Explain why.

4   Which kind of molecules:

    a   can pass into your blood?

    b   cannot pass into your blood?

    Explain your answers.

5   Write down <u>three</u> substances that you can absorb without
    digesting them.

8A.5

1   List, in order, the parts of your digestive system that your food
    travels through.

2   a   What happened to the meat in the wooden blocks that
        Spallanzani swallowed?

    b   Where did this happen?

continued

3 Choose the correct conclusion (A–D) for Spallanzani's experiments.

A Meat breaks down to amino acids in the stomach.

B The juices in the stomach break down meat.

C Proteins break down into amino acids that can be absorbed.

D Meat is broken down entirely in the stomach.

4 Proteins break down into amino acids.
Draw a diagram to show what the protein in the diagram looks like when it is broken down.

5 Write down <u>two</u> things that scientists have found out about enzymes.

6 **a** Find out the connection between an endoscope, fibre optics and a stomach ulcer.

b Find out <u>one</u> reason why doctors take X-rays of a patient's digestive system.

In your group, agree on a few sentences about each of **a** and **b**.

7 To find out what is wrong with a patient, doctors use tests and tools. These are developed and used by various specialist scientists working together with doctors.

a Find out what specialisms were involved in the development of either X-rays or endoscopes. Combine the group's ideas into a list.

b Sharing ideas and collaborating are important in science. In your group, discuss the reasons.

8A.6

1 What kind of substance can you put in the Visking tubing to break down the starch into sugar?

2 What happens to the sugar that is made?

3 Your saliva breaks down starch.
What does this tell you about your saliva?

4 Think carefully of ways in which the model is different from a real small intestine.
Write down your answers.

5 Write down a list of nutrients that can pass into your blood.

6 Write down <u>two</u> groups of nutrients that you don't need to digest.

7 Describe <u>two</u> things that can happen to sugars after they pass into the blood.

8 Write down <u>one</u> kind of cell that uses lots of sugars.
Explain your answer.

You should already know

Outcomes

Keywords

Your cells use food as a source of materials to grow, and for energy.

You use energy for moving, growing and keeping warm.

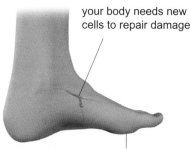

your body needs new cells to repair damage

skin cells have to be replaced as they get worn away

You need glucose for energy and amino acids to make proteins for new cells.

Gail's muscle cells use up more glucose to release extra energy when she runs.

This is a high-energy drink for sports players. It contains a lot of glucose.

Question 1 2 3 4

Releasing energy

Glucose supplies your cells with **energy**. You could say that glucose is your body's fuel. But you don't burn glucose. Chemical reactions in your cells break it down to release the energy a bit at a time. We call this **respiration**. Respiration takes place in every cell in your body. Because your cells normally use **oxygen** from the air when they respire, we call this **aerobic** respiration.

The word equation for aerobic respiration is:

fuel

oxygen

ENERGY

In cars and lorries, fuel is burnt in oxygen to release energy. Your cells also use oxygen to release energy from their fuel.

> glucose + oxygen ⟶ **carbon dioxide** + water + energy

The word equation doesn't show that the glucose breaks down a bit at a time. It just shows the reactants and the products.

Question 5 6

How oxygen reaches your tissues

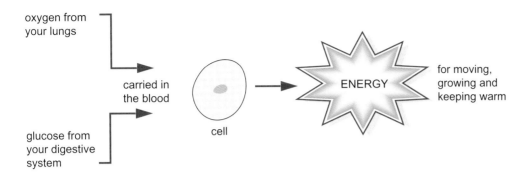

All your cells use oxygen to release energy from glucose. Air contains oxygen. You take air into and out of your lungs. This is called **breathing**. Some of the oxygen from the air in your lungs passes into your blood.

Your blood then carries the oxygen to your tissues. It passes out of your blood into the **tissue fluid** (a liquid that surrounds all cells). Then it passes into your cells.

Question 7 8 9

More about exchanges

Substances are passing in and out of your blood and your cells all the time. In Unit 7G, you learnt how substances diffuse from where they are in high concentration to where they are in low concentration. We say that substances pass in and out of cells by **diffusion**.

In your tissues, oxygen and glucose diffuse into your cells. Carbon dioxide diffuses out of your cells into the tissue fluid.

In your lungs, oxygen goes into your blood and carbon dioxide leaves it and goes into the air in your lungs. When you breathe out, you get rid of this extra carbon dioxide.

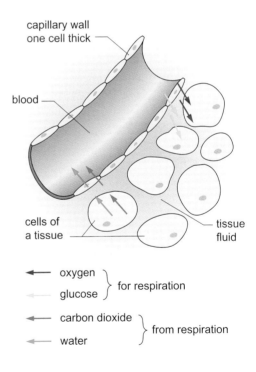

Exchange of materials between cells and the blood.

Question 10 11

You should already know | Outcomes | Keywords

The story of blood circulation

In the 2nd century BC, the Chinese knew about the circulation of the blood. Travellers brought the idea to Europe but it was lost. The ancient Greeks and Romans thought that blood moved back and forth like the tides in the sea. In the 13th century AD, an Arab doctor called Ibn al-Nafis (also known as Al-Quarashi) worked out the circulation of blood through the **heart** and lungs. His work was translated into Latin in the 16th century. Also in that century, a Spanish doctor called Michael Servetus wrote about blood flow through the heart and lungs.

In the 17th century, a British scientist called William Harvey observed the hearts of many different mammals. He compared the working of hearts and pumps. He also measured the amount of blood leaving the heart. His observations and experiments provided **evidence** for the circulation of blood. Harvey also predicted the discovery of tiny vessels between arteries and veins. But he couldn't see them.

The diagram shows Harvey's experiment which showed that blood travels in one direction in veins.

William Harvey is often credited with the discovery of the double circulation of blood through the heart.

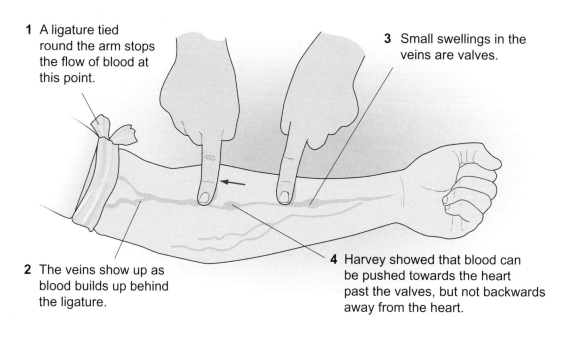

1 A ligature tied round the arm stops the flow of blood at this point.

3 Small swellings in the veins are valves.

2 The veins show up as blood builds up behind the ligature.

4 Harvey showed that blood can be pushed towards the heart past the valves, but not backwards away from the heart.

Question 1 / 2 / 3

Finding the link between arteries and veins

An Italian scientist called Marcello Malpighi discovered the tiny vessels that link arteries and veins some years later. We call them **capillaries**. They are about 0.01 mm wide.

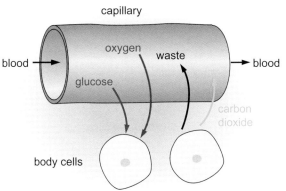

Exchanging substances at the capillaries. No cell is far from a capillary.

Now we know a lot more

Malpighi knew that blood left the heart in **arteries**, that arteries split up into tiny tubes called capillaries in your tissues and that capillaries join up to form **veins** that take blood back to your heart.

We now know that capillaries are important because this is where substances go in and out of your blood.

Your heart

Your heart is a muscular pump. Heart muscles squeeze blood to move it around your body. The two sides of your heart pump blood out at the same time. Because of this, we say that it acts like a double pump.

This photo of capillaries was taken using a modern microscope. Capillary walls are only one cell thick.

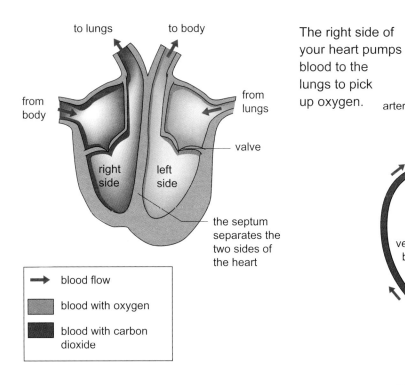

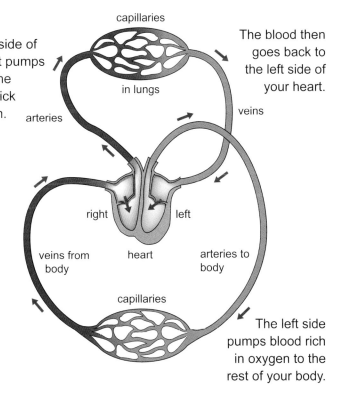

The blood system, showing the double circulation.

Aerobic respiration in cells

Aerobic respiration is a series of chemical reactions. It happens in every cell.

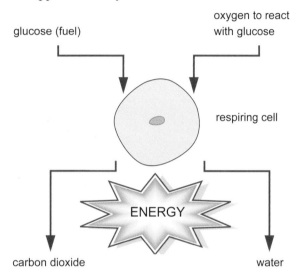

glucose (fuel)

oxygen to react with glucose

respiring cell

ENERGY

carbon dioxide

water

An aerobics exercise class.

Question 1 2

Sometimes there isn't enough oxygen in the air

The climber in the photograph is working at 4500 m above sea level. At high altitudes like this, the air molecules are more spread out. The climber is taking in less **oxygen** than normal with each breath. So his blood cannot supply his cells with all the oxygen they need.

Question 3 4

At high altitudes, the air in a passenger aeroplane is kept pressurised. This means that the amount of oxygen in the air is similar to that near the ground.

Question 5

Lack of oxygen leads to tiredness, a bad headache and difficulty in concentrating.

Sometimes lung damage reduces oxygen uptake

Lung tissue is thin and delicate, and so it is easily damaged.
The more it is damaged, the smaller the surface area of the lungs.
This means that less oxygen can diffuse into the blood.

> Jack's story
>
> I spent 25 years working in a coal mine. As a result of breathing in dust for many years, I developed a bad cough, then miner's lung (pneumoconiosis). The stretchy tissue inside my lungs was damaged. It was being replaced with fibrous tissue that didn't let my lungs stretch as I breathed in.
>
> I was finding it harder and harder to breathe and had to give up work. Now I have to use oxygen from a cylinder. I am so short of breath that I can only walk about 100 metres. We didn't have dust masks in my day.

Question 6 **7**

Smoking also damages the lungs

Smokers often cough, because tobacco smoke irritates their air passages. Coughing damages the delicate tissue in the lungs. People with damaged lungs get out of breath easily. They can't take in enough oxygen.

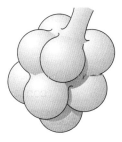

Healthy lung tissue.

Damaged lung tissue.

Question 8 **9**

Check your progress

You should already know | Outcomes | Keywords

Obtaining oxygen, getting rid of carbon dioxide

In Topic 8B.3, you found out why your **lungs** are so important and why they are so easily damaged.

Remember that you get the oxygen you need from the air. You **breathe** air in and out of your lungs. In your lungs, oxygen from the air diffuses into your blood. At the same time, waste carbon dioxide passes from your blood into the air. We call this **gas exchange**.

The air that you breathe out contains the waste carbon dioxide from respiration. So there is <u>less</u> oxygen and <u>more</u> carbon dioxide in the air that you breathe <u>out</u> than in the air that you breathe <u>in</u>.

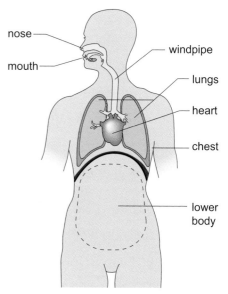

Air passages to the lungs.

Question 1 / 2

How gas exchange happens

Inside the lungs are millions of tiny air sacs called **alveoli**. Alveoli give the lungs a spongy feel and a very large surface area.

The walls of alveoli are only one cell thick. The very large number of capillaries around the alveoli give the lungs their pink colour. Capillary walls are also just one cell thick. So gases can pass quickly between the air in the alveoli and the blood in the capillaries.

Blood carries oxygen away continuously from the alveoli to supply the body cells. It also continuously brings waste carbon dioxide from the body cells to the alveoli. This prevents carbon dioxide building up in your blood and poisoning you. You get rid of the carbon dioxide in the air that you breathe out.

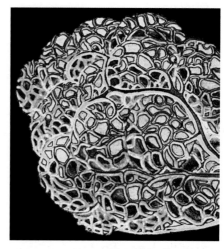

Alveoli in the lungs.

Question 3 / 4 / 5

So the stages in getting oxygen to your cells and getting rid of carbon dioxide are as follows.

- **Breathing**

  You breathe air into and out of your lungs.

- **Gas exchange**

  Gases are exchanged between the air in the alveoli and the blood.

- **Transport**

  Transport of gases between the capillaries in the lungs and the cells.

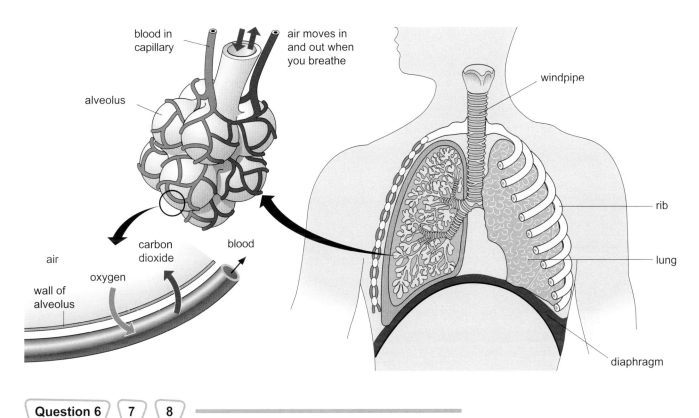

Question 6 **7** **8**

Smoking affects …

… gas exchange

You already know that coughing damages alveoli and reduces the surface area of the lungs. So, less oxygen passes into the blood.

… transport of oxygen

Red blood cells carry the oxygen in blood. But they carry carbon monoxide even more easily. Tobacco smoke contains carbon monoxide. So, on average, smokers and people who breathe in a lot of tobacco smoke (passive smokers) can carry less oxygen in their blood than non-smokers do.

Question 9 **10**

You should already know | Outcomes | Keywords

Investigating diseases

When there is an outbreak of an infection such as cholera, doctors work with public health officials to find out where the bacteria came from. When people work together like this, we say that they **collaborate**.

The study of the causes of diseases in populations is called **epidemiology**. Diseases such as heart disease, lung disease and cancer have many causes. Doctors want to know the main causes so that they can work to prevent these diseases. So they gather data about medical histories and lifestyle. Then statisticians help them to analyse the data. They look for factors with links to the disease. We call these **risk factors**. To prove that it causes a disease, they need to find out how a risk factor causes that disease. They have shown how tobacco smoke causes cancers.

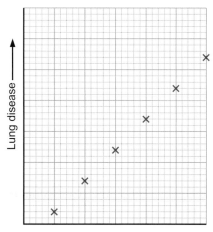

This graph shows the kind of link that researchers look for. It shows that mining <u>might be</u> a **cause** of lung disease.

Question 1 / 2

Worldwide collaboration

The World Health Organisation (WHO) coordinates worldwide health matters within the United Nations. Lung disease is a worldwide problem.

The WHO is coordinating work on lung disease by institutions, doctors, health educators, scientists and statisticians from around the world. They are:

- gathering and analysing more data;
- looking at recent epidemiological study methods to try to develop standard methods for future research. If the methods in different countries are the same, data can be combined.
- providing evidence for policies for health improvement and support to carry them out.

So, by collaborating, they hope to change things more quickly.

Risk factors for lung disease

- Smoking tobacco, including passive smoking.
- Breathing in dust and chemicals at work.
- Indoor air pollution, e.g. from open fires.
- Outdoor air pollution.
- Frequent respiratory infections in childhood.

Worldwide data

Doctors now group lung diseases together as:

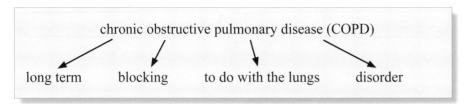

The data brought together by the WHO shows that, worldwide:

- over three million people die from lung diseases every year – this is about 5% of all deaths;
- over 90% of deaths from COPD are in poorer countries;
- 80 million people are <u>known</u> to have moderate to severe COPD (six hundred thousand of them in the UK);
- millions more have COPD but <u>don't know</u> it; most are not diagnosed before the age of 40;
- COPD affects men and women equally.

Factfile

COPD includes

- chronic bronchitis
- emphysema
- asbestosis
- pneumoconiosis
- tumours

Signs and symptoms

- shortness of breath
- coughing and phlegm
- bluish skin (lack of oxygen)

Question 3   4   5

The WHO is working with organisations to reduce the risk factors that people are exposed to, such as:

- tobacco smoke;
- factory and mine dust;
- particulates such as soot.

Reducing smoking and air pollution will reduce lung disease and its impact on families, communities and the economy.

It will take many years for this work to have an effect. But we must do something.

If we don't, the WHO suggests that deaths from COPD will increase by more than 30% in the next 10 years. Absence from work owing to COPD will also increase.

Question 6   7   8

Open fires for cooking cause indoor air pollution.

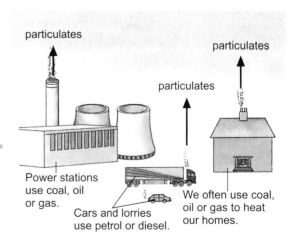

Particulates such as soot from vehicles and industry cause outdoor air pollution that can affect our lungs.

8B.5 Comparing inhaled and exhaled air

You should already know

Outcomes

Keywords

Respiration makes waste products

Look, when you breathe out onto this mirror, it steps up.

It's like when you breathe out on a cold day – you can see your breath.

Question 1   2   3

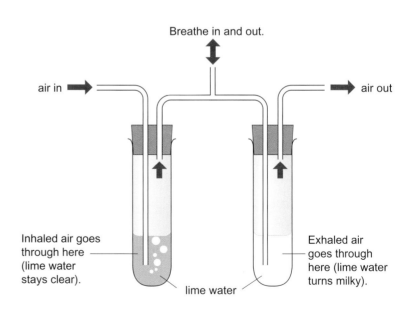

Breathe in and out.

air in → → air out

Inhaled air goes through here (lime water stays clear).

Exhaled air goes through here (lime water turns milky).

lime water

All cells make waste products when they respire. The waste products of aerobic respiration are **water** and **carbon dioxide**. Carbon dioxide is poisonous so you get rid of it in the air you exhale (breathe out).

Comparing the amounts of carbon dioxide in inhaled and exhaled air.

Question 4

Peter did an experiment to compare the amounts of gases in air breathed in and out. Look at his results.

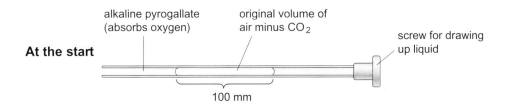

At the start

alkaline pyrogallate (absorbs oxygen)

original volume of air minus CO_2

screw for drawing up liquid

100 mm

After 40 minutes

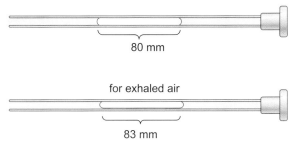

80 mm

for exhaled air

83 mm

Gas	Air breathed in (%)	Air breathed out (%)
oxygen	21	17
carbon dioxide	0.03	4
nitrogen	79	79
water vapour	varies	saturated

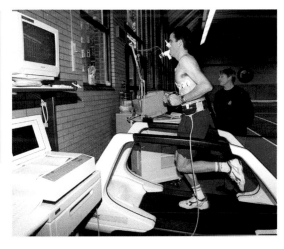

This athlete is measuring the gases in his exhaled air.

Question 6 7 8 9

You should already know ⟩   ⟨ Outcomes ⟩   ⟨ Keywords ⟩

Finding evidence for respiration

The cells of all living things need to release **energy** to carry out their life processes. Most of them use oxygen and produce **carbon dioxide**.

Carbon dioxide production is a good way of finding out if **respiration** is happening.

When you breathe in and out through lime water, you find that the air you breathe out contains a lot more carbon dioxide than the air you breathe in. But you can't ask a seed or a woodlouse to breathe in and out!

The diagrams show two experiments that you can do.

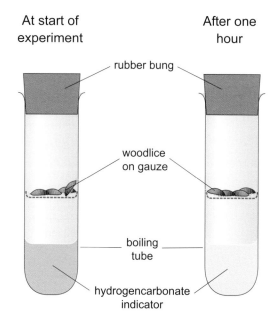

Experiment 1

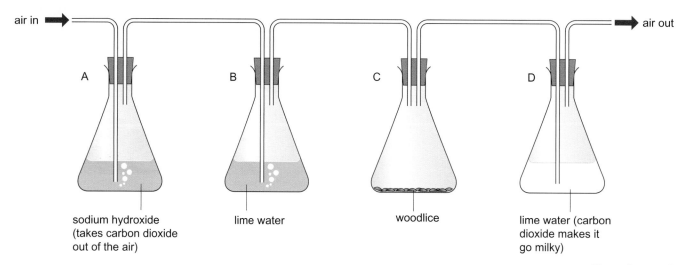

Experiment 2

Question 1 ⟩ 2 ⟩ 3 ⟩

In experiment 2

The first flask of lime water (flask B) shows that the air reaching the woodlice has no carbon dioxide in it.

We need flask B to show that the carbon dioxide in flask D can have come only from the woodlice and anything living in or on them.

In experiment 1

We use one tube with and one tube without woodlice.
Then we can say that the woodlice cause any change. We call the second tube the **control**.

Without the control, we can argue that something else might have caused the change. Carbon dioxide could have leaked into the tube. Light, temperature differences or anything else could have caused the change.

Question 4   5   6

Things to remember when you design experiments using living things

Remember that <u>all</u> living things respire.

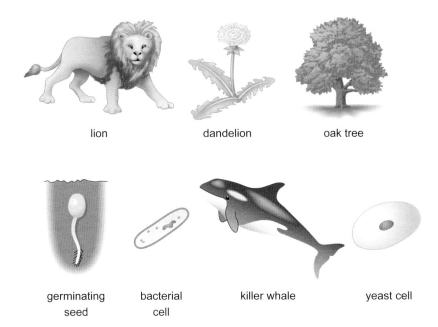

lion   dandelion   oak tree

germinating   bacterial   killer whale   yeast cell
seed   cell

- Use more than one living thing, because living things vary.
- Use a control so that any change can be caused only by the variable that you are testing – it can't be caused by light, temperature or any other variable.
- Vary only one thing at a time.
- Treat living things with care and sensitivity.

Review your work

Summary ➡

8B.1

1 Write down <u>one</u> food that provides energy for cells.

2 Write down <u>two</u> reasons why you need to make new cells.

3 Write down <u>one</u> time when your muscle cells need more glucose than normal.

4 People doing sports often use high-energy drinks. A slice of bread contains just as much energy as 200 cm³ of the drink. Why is the energy in the drink more useful than the energy in the bread during exercise?

5 What is respiration?

6 Write down:

    a <u>two</u> things that cells need for respiration;

    b how these things get to your cells;

    c <u>two</u> waste substances that are produced in respiration.

7 Draw a flow diagram to show how oxygen gets from the air to the cells in the body.

8 Why do all the tissues in the body need blood vessels near them?

9 Some parts of the body have a better blood supply than others.

    Explain why the following organs need to have plenty of blood vessels:

    a muscles;

    b the lining of the uterus of a pregnant woman.

10 Write down <u>two</u> materials that diffuse:

    a from your blood to your cells;

    b from your cells into your blood.

11 Why do you need tissue fluid?

8B.2

1 Draw a time line to show how ideas about blood circulation changed.

2 Harvey did not find the tiny vessels that link arteries and veins.
Suggest why.

3 What technology was needed before capillaries could be discovered?

4 Draw a simple flow chart to show what Harvey and Malpighi found.

5 What have modern scientists learnt from Harvey about studying the human body?

6 Use books or the Internet to find out more about the contribution made by <u>one</u> of the following to the story of blood circulation:

- the ancient Chinese;
- the ancient Greeks (including scientists like Galen of Pergamum and Erasistratus);
- Islamic science (including scientists like Ibn-al-Nafis / Al-Quarashi);
- Michael Servetus.

Agree in your group how to present the information.

continued

7   Write down <u>one</u> reason why substances pass into and out of capillaries easily.

8   There are blood capillaries close to all the cells in all your organs, including your lungs.
    Why is this?

9   What is your heart mainly made from?

10 Why does your heart need lots of glucose and oxygen?

11 Look at the diagram of the double circulation of the blood.
    Write down, in order, the parts that the blood goes through. Start and finish at the right side of the heart.

12 How many times does blood pass through your heart each time it does a full circuit of your body?

13 The wall of the left side of the heart is thicker than the wall of the right side.
    Suggest why.

8B.3

1   Write down the word equation for respiration to remind yourself of what happens.

2   How do you think the amount of energy available is affected if there isn't enough:
    a   glucose?
    b   oxygen?

3   What are the symptoms of altitude sickness?

4   The climber's cells are not getting enough oxygen.
    Explain why this makes him feel tired.

5   If the amount of oxygen in the air drops slightly, pilots notice that their judgement and ability to concentrate are not as good.
    Why do you think this is?

6   Explain why Jack found it hard to breathe.

7   There are many jobs in which people should wear dust masks.
    Suggest <u>two</u> of these jobs.

8   Explain why people with damaged lung tissue easily get out of breath.

9   Find out about the cause and symptoms of <u>one</u> other lung condition. Make brief notes.
    Remember to write down where you found your information.

8B.4

1 Look at the diagram.
   Draw a flow chart to show the route air takes to get into your lungs.

2 What happens during gas exchange?

3 Write down <u>two</u> reasons why it is important that gas exchange happens very quickly.

4 In what way are lungs arranged so that they have a large surface area?

5 Why does a large surface area help gas exchange happen quickly?

6 Why do thin walls help gas exchange happen quickly?

7 Why can substances pass in and out of capillaries easily?

8 There are a lot of capillaries around the alveoli.
   How does this help gas exchange?

9 Smoking affects the amount of oxygen that reaches your cells.
   Write down <u>two</u> reasons.

10 Sports coaches ask the people that they train not to smoke because of the effects on their performance and on their general health.
   Suggest why not smoking benefits:
   a   their sporting performance;
   b   their health.

8B.HSW

1 What does the term <u>collaborate</u> mean?

2 List <u>four</u> risk factors for lung diseases.

3 In your group, gather suggestions about the following questions.
   In the fight against COPD in the UK:
   a   which agencies need to collaborate?
   b   what kinds of specialist need to be involved?

4 Out of 100 people who die next year, how many are likely to die from COPD?

5 What percentage of people in the better-off countries die from COPD?

6 What is the main risk factor for lung disease?

7 Suggest why it will probably take many years to reduce the number of deaths from lung disease.

continued

8 In the UK, 7% of sickness-related days off work are due to COPD. This is not just bad for the people who are ill.

In your group, discuss some of the effects of people's absence from work:

  a on their families;

  b on other people in their workplace;

  c on the country.

8B.5

1 What is the liquid on the mirror?

2 Where does it come from?

3 Why does water vapour show up in exhaled air on a cold day?

4 What are the <u>two</u> waste products of aerobic respiration?

5 **a** Which contains more oxygen – inhaled or exhaled air?

  b Explain why this is.

6 Which gas is always more abundant in exhaled air than inhaled air?

7 Where is this extra gas made?

8 The amount of water vapour in inhaled air varies. Why is this?

9 The runner in the photograph is making more carbon dioxide than he does when he is asleep. Explain why that is.

8B.6

1 **a** Write down <u>two</u> substances that you can use to detect carbon dioxide.

  b Describe the change to each substance when carbon dioxide is present.

2 In experiment 2, the woodlice breathe in air that has no carbon dioxide in it. How do you know?

3 The change in the lime water shows that there is carbon dioxide in the air going through flask D. Where did it come from?

4 Describe the results of experiment 1.

5 What can you conclude from experiment 1?

6 Katie did an experiment like this with maggots. But she didn't use a second tube. The indicator changed colour. Her teacher told her that she couldn't conclude that maggots produced carbon dioxide. Why is this?

8C.1 Micro-organisms and how to grow them (HSW)

You should already know | **Outcomes** | **Keywords**

Types of micro-organism

Some living things are so small that we can only see them through a microscope. We call these tiny living things **micro-organisms** or microbes. They include **viruses** and **bacteria,** and some **fungi**.

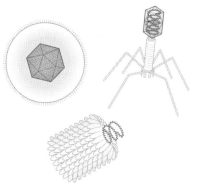

Examples of viruses

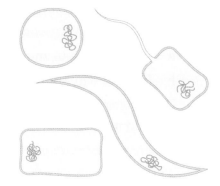

Examples of bacteria

Yeast is a fungus that we use for making bread and wine. It is made of single cells that reproduce by budding off new cells.

Moulds are thread-like fungi. Some cause decay. We use others for making antibiotics.

Fungi include yeasts and moulds. We use them to make bread, beer and cheese. Althlete's foot is a disease caused by a fungus.

Question 1

There are lots of different types of micro-organism. Although they are very small, they have a huge effect on our lives. Micro-organisms are an essential part of life on Earth. Some are very useful. Others cause **disease**.

Question 2

Here are two micro-organism fact files.

FACT FILE: Viruses

Average size	0.0001 mm
Structure	A strand of genetic material wrapped in a protein coat.
Found	Viruses can reproduce only inside living cells.
Uses	To kill pest animals.
Diseases	Common cold, influenza (flu), measles, AIDS, yellow fever, rabies. Viruses cause disease in animals, plants and even other micro-organisms.

FACT FILE: Bacteria

Average size	0.001 mm
Structure	Bacteria are single-celled with a strong cell wall. Their genetic material is not in a nucleus.
Found	Most bacteria live in water, soil and decaying matter.
Uses	To make yoghurt, cheese and vinegar.
Diseases	Typhoid, cholera, food poisoning.

Question 3 **4** **5** **6**

How to grow micro-organisms

Yeast is the most commonly grown micro-organism in the world. We use it to make beer, wine and bread. Yeast is a living thing, so it needs warmth and food to grow.

Just like all living things, yeast breaks down food to get energy. We call this process **respiration**. If it uses oxygen, we call it **aerobic respiration**. But yeast can also respire without oxygen, and we call this **anaerobic respiration**. When it does this it makes alcohol. In both cases, it produces carbon dioxide.

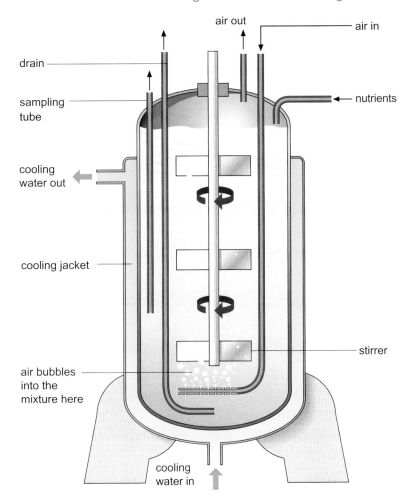

This is how yeast is grown on a large scale. Each vat is big enough to fit a family car inside!

Question 7 **8**

Bread dough is made with yeast, flour, water and a little sugar and salt. Laura did an experiment to see whether sugar helps dough rise. She measured the amount of dough in each measuring cylinder after 30 minutes.

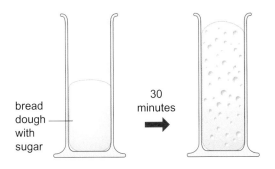

Amount of sugar in the dough in g	Volume of the dough after 30 minutes in cm^3
0	40
5	52
10	66
15	74
20	80

Question 9 **10** **11**

Yeast is just one type of fungus. We can also grow other fungi in large vats to make useful products.

Product made by fungi	Use
penicillin	an antibiotic to treat some diseases
citric acid	added to make soft drinks taste tangy
cortisone	to treat arthritis
pectinase	added to fruit juice to make it clear
mycoprotein	a substitute for meat that is suitable for vegetarians (for example, Quorn®)

Question 12

Growing micro-organisms in a laboratory

In a laboratory, we grow bacteria in Petri dishes – small plastic or glass dishes with lids. Food for the bacteria is mixed with a jelly called agar, which is made from seaweed. Each type of micro-organism needs its own particular balance of minerals and food to grow.

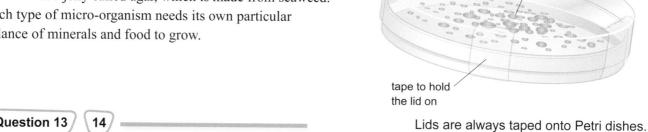

agar jelly   colony of bacteria (a group of thousands of bacteria)

tape to hold the lid on

Lids are always taped onto Petri dishes.

Question 13 **14**

We must clean everything we use to grow micro-organisms before it is used. Petri dishes and agar are heated to over 100 °C to sterilise them. It is important to keep all benches and equipment clean.

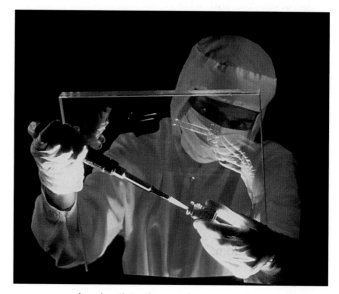

A scientist who works with micro-organisms is called a microbiologist.

Question 15 **16**

John Snow's evidence

- Most people who died lived very near to the Broad Street pump.
- Only 5 out of 500 people died at the workhouse round the corner from the pump. The workhouse had its own well.
- No one in the local brewery died. All the workers drank beer instead of water.
- Two ladies who lived 5 miles away died of cholera. They had a bottle of water brought to them from the Broad Street pump because they liked the taste.

By the 7th of September three-quarters of the people living in Soho had fled the area. Many of those who remained were ill and 28 more died that day.

John Snow put his evidence to the Parish Board and they agreed to remove the handle of the pump the next day. People could no longer drink the water. The number of new cases began to fall.

Question 3

A few months later John Snow found the cause of the epidemic.

- Water for the pump came from an underground well.
- Number 40 Broad Street had an underground cesspit for sewage.
- During August, a baby at number 40 was ill with cholera, and his mother washed his nappies in water that she then tipped into the cesspit.
- The cesspit wall was cracked and the sewage leaked out into the nearby well.
- This allowed the bacteria that cause cholera to reach the Broad Street pump.

Question 4

Check your progress

8C.4 Protecting ourselves against disease

You should already know   Outcomes   Keywords

Your body's defences

Look at the drawing.

Question 1 2 3

Each time people cough or sneeze, they spray little droplets into the air.

Someone with tuberculosis (TB) coughs out TB **bacteria**. TB is a serious **disease** that destroys lung tissue and kills if not treated.

Droplets sneezed out by people with colds contain thousands of **viruses**.

If you are nearby, you can breathe them in. Sometimes they get past the defences in your air passages and into your lungs.

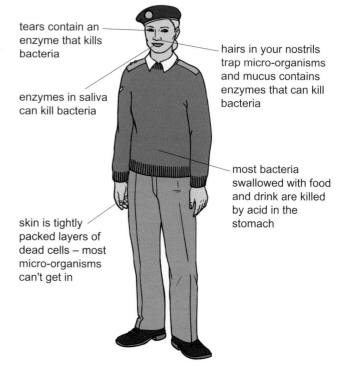

tears contain an enzyme that kills bacteria

hairs in your nostrils trap micro-organisms and mucus contains enzymes that can kill bacteria

enzymes in saliva can kill bacteria

most bacteria swallowed with food and drink are killed by acid in the stomach

skin is tightly packed layers of dead cells – most micro-organisms can't get in

Question 4 5

How your body defends itself against micro-organisms. Unfortunately, micro-organisms get past these defences.

Antibiotics help to fight some diseases

Antibiotics are substances made by living things. They can kill some other living things. Antibiotics kill bacteria but not viruses.

For centuries, people knew that spreading mould on a wound sometimes helped it to heal. Scientists noticed that some moulds stop bacteria growing. But they didn't realise that this was important.

In 1928, some spores of mould landed on one of Alexander Fleming's Petri dishes of bacteria. He noticed that there were no bacteria where the mould grew. The mould had made a substance that stopped the bacteria growing. The mould was called *Penicillium* so Fleming named the substance **penicillin**. It was first used in 1942 and, since then, its use has saved millions of lives.

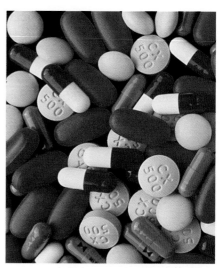

Penicillin kills only some kinds of bacteria. We now have lots of different antibiotics to treat different infections.

Question 6 7 8 9 10 11

How your body destroys micro-organisms

Your blood contains red blood cells and **white blood cells**. There are two different types of white blood cell.

- One type engulfs (traps) micro-organisms and destroys them.
- The other type makes substances called **antibodies**. These stop micro-organisms working properly.

Each antibody that you make acts against only one type of micro-organism. So you need different antibodies against different micro-organisms. It takes time for your body to make new kinds of antibodies. So, you feel ill until you have made enough of the right antibodies to destroy the micro-organisms.

Once you have had a disease, your white blood cells are able to make antibodies against it. If a second attack comes, your body can destroy the micro-organisms before they have time to make you ill. This means that you are immune to the disease. You have **immunity**.

There is a problem with colds and flu – these viruses change all the time. Your white blood cells don't recognise new forms of these viruses.

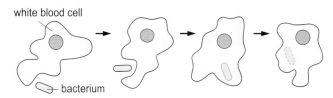

Some white blood cells take in micro-organisms and destroy them.

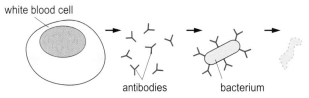

Some white blood cells make antibodies that stop micro-organisms working properly.

Jabs can also make you immune to a particular disease

A jab is an injection of a **vaccine**. This makes you immune to the disease. So we call having a jab **immunisation**.

Question 15

Your tuberculosis (TB) jab is just one of 11 injections you may have during your childhood. The vaccine in a TB jab contains a weakened form of the bacteria that cause tuberculosis. The vaccine has the same effect on your immune system as being infected with TB but you won't be ill. Your arm may feel sore.

In future, your white blood cells will be able to make the right antibodies much more quickly. So if TB bacteria get into your body, you will make antibodies to destroy them and not become ill.

Before scientists developed the TB jab, the only way you could be immune to TB was by surviving the disease. A jab makes you immune without having the disease itself.

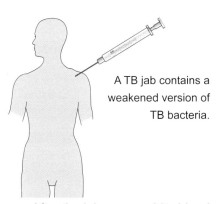

A TB jab contains a weakened version of TB bacteria.

After the jab, some white blood cells make the right antibodies to kill TB bacteria.

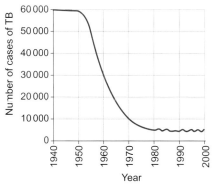

Total annual number of cases of TB in England and Wales, from 1940 to 2000. (From the Public Health Laboratory Service.)

Review your work

Summary ➡

You should already know | Outcomes | Keywords

Using ideas from the past

Sometimes people stop using a common remedy, and then doctors find that it had its uses after all.

4000 years ago, the Egyptians used honey to treat infected wounds. They didn't know why it worked. Modern doctors researched the idea, and found out that honey slows the growth of bacteria. So they are testing new ways of using it.

Question 1 2 3

This modern dressing for infected wounds contains honey.

Leeches past and present

In ancient Egypt, Greece and Rome, physicians used leeches to take blood from their patients. This is called blood-letting. In Egypt, they thought that blood-letting removed the 'blockages' in the body that caused disease. The Greeks thought that excess blood caused some diseases and used leeches to remove it.

Treatment with leeches continued for centuries. Doctors were even known as 'leeches'. William Harvey, who discovered blood circulation, wrote:

> daily experience satisfies us that blood-letting
> has a most salutary effect in many diseases.

Doctors kept leeches in jars. Sometimes, their patients recovered after blood-letting. Sometimes, they died.

As doctors found out more about the causes of illness and researched treatments to find out which worked best, they used leeches to treat fewer and fewer illnesses. In the 1860s, London hospitals used about seven million leeches a year. By the 1930s, most hospitals had stopped using them.

Question 4 5 6 7

Doctors are now using leeches again. They know now that leech saliva contains substances that not only stop blood clotting but also dissolve blood clots. They are making use of these properties.

Look at the Fact file.

Question 8 9

Fact file

Now doctors use leeches to:

- thin the blood to prevent clotting after heart surgery;
- dissolve blood clots – in major blood vessels, clots can kill;
- unblock tiny blood vessels following microsurgery such as sewing on chopped-off fingers;
- reduce bruising after surgery.

Maggots in and out of use

Surgeons in Napoleon's armies noticed that, if soldiers had blowfly maggots in their wounds:

- their wounds healed more quickly;
- they were less likely to die from infection.

By the time of the American Civil War, surgeons were actually putting maggots into wounds. But they didn't know why this worked and it fell out of use. Later, doctors used antibiotics against infections instead of maggots.

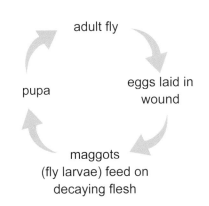

Then researchers looked at the evidence about maggots again. They found out how they worked. So they are using them again – up to 200 maggots in one wound. Maggots clean a wound or an ulcer in about 5 days. Other treatments take up to 18 times as long. Using maggots could save the NHS tens of millions of pounds a year.

Some doctors think that maggots may turn out to be the best treatment for wounds infected with MRSA. This bacterium is sometimes called a 'superbug' because it is resistant to many antibiotics and it kills about one in five of infected people.

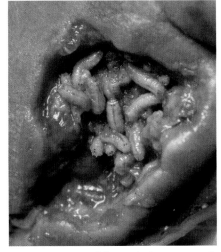

Maggots in a wound.

Another look at bacteriophages

Look at the picture. When scientists discovered **bacteriophages** (also called **phages**), they thought that they had discovered a possible cure for bacterial infection. First, however, they had to solve a problem – each kind kills only one kind of bacterium.

The Russians found a phage that killed the bacteria that cause gangrene. They treated infected soldiers with it during the Second World War. Now they are using a different phage to treat sore throats.

In the West, scientists focused on the development of antibiotics. Now they are looking at phages again. In the UK, one company is developing a cream containing phages. It's designed to kill MRSA inside the nose so that it doesn't get into wounds. Other researchers are looking at sprays to use on meat to kill the bacteria that cause food poisoning.

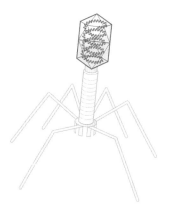

Bacteriophages (or phages) are **viruses** that kill bacteria.

So, in the past, honey, leeches, maggots and phages were all used with mixed success. They all went out of favour – but they are all being investigated again.

8C.1

1 Write down <u>three</u> different types of micro-organism.

2 Write down <u>two</u> things we make using micro-organisms.

3 How many times bigger is the average bacterium than the average virus?

4 Which type of micro-organism is the smallest?

5 Which <u>two</u> types of micro-organism make food rot?

6 Make a table of information about viruses, bacteria and fungi.

7 Write down <u>three</u> things that both yeast and humans do.

8 The yeast cells in this vat respire aerobically.
What is the evidence for this in the design of the vat?

9 How does the amount of sugar affect how high the dough rises?

10 What is the gas that makes dough rise?

11 When making bread, you leave the dough to rise for several hours.
Then you bake it for 30 minutes at 200 °C.
What do you think happens to yeast during baking? (Remember, yeast is a living thing.)

12 Look at the table.
Write down <u>two</u> medicines made by fungi.

13 Bacteria are so small that you can only see them with a microscope.
Why can you see bacteria growing on agar?

14 Why do you think the dishes used to grow bacteria are also called agar plates?

15 Look at the photograph.
Write down <u>three</u> things the worker is wearing to prevent any unwanted micro-organisms from contaminating his work.

16 What do you think would happen if laboratory workers did not sterilise the equipment properly?

8C.2

1   How can a child at a birthday party give all the other children chickenpox?

2   Why is it important that you wash your hands before you prepare food?

3   How could you stop food poisoning being spread by flies?

4   Write down <u>one</u> way of making water safe to drink.

5   Write down <u>two</u> ways that a mother can pass on a disease to her baby.

8C.3

1   How many people died from cholera in the first three days of the epidemic?

2   Suggest who could have collected the data that alerted John Snow.

3   Imagine you are the person who took the handle off the pump.
A crowd of local people complain because they now have to walk 10 minutes to get drinking water.
In your group, discuss what to say to them.

4   John Snow could not see the bacteria that cause cholera.
How could he be sure there were bacteria in the well of the Broad Street pump?

8C.4

1   Why can't micro-organisms normally get into your body through your skin?

2   In which part of your body are micro-organisms killed by acid?

3   Animals often lick their wounds.
How does this help them to heal?

4   Why are you less likely to catch TB if you breathe through your nose rather than through your mouth?

5   Why should you cover your nose and mouth when you sneeze?

6   Would you put mouldy food on a cut to help it to heal?
Discuss this in your group.

7   What stops bacteria from growing close to *Penicillium*?

8   Normally, new drugs are tested and trialled for years before they are widely used. Doctors used penicillin as soon as it could be made in large quantities.
Suggest why.
(Hint: the Second World War was from 1939 to 1945.)

continued

9 Before penicillin was discovered, one in three people who caught pneumonia died. When penicillin was used, only one in 20 people died.

If 300 people caught pneumonia, how many would probably have died:

a before penicillin was discovered?

b after penicillin was discovered?

10 The discovery and development of penicillin is an interesting story.

a Find out more about it, in particular the work of Howard Florey and Ernst Chain.

b In your group, discuss what the story of penicillin tells us about the way scientific knowledge can develop.

11 Mrs Sharples has flu (caused by a virus).
She wants antibiotics to make her better.
What would you tell her?

12 Why don't you usually catch the same disease twice?

13 When you have had a cold you become immune to that particular virus.
How is it that, a few months later, you can catch another cold?

14 Breast milk contains the mother's antibodies.
How does this stop a breast-fed baby from catching some diseases?

15 Find out what vaccinations you have had and when you had them.

16 Why do your white blood cells make antibodies in response to the TB vaccine?

17 Draw a flow chart to show how the TB immunisation stops you catching TB.

18 Look at the graph.
What year do you think TB jabs were first introduced as a routine immunisation for all children in England and Wales?

19 In the year 2000, there were still over 6000 cases of TB in England and Wales. Not everyone is immunised against TB.
Write down two possible reasons why someone might not have had the TB jab.

20 Vaccination doesn't just protect you. When most people are vaccinated, the population is protected against an outbreak.
Suggest why.

8C.HSW

1   Look at the picture.
    What use of honey does it show?

2   Some people use Manuka honey.
    Find out what they use it for.

3   In your group, discuss possible reasons why modern doctors started
    to research the use of honey.

4   In your group, take a vote on whether you are willing to be treated
    using leeches and maggots.

5   Explain in your own words what Harvey thought about the use
    of leeches.

6   Too much blood-letting makes people more ill.
    In your group, discuss possible explanations.

7   In your group, discuss why the use of leeches went out of favour.

8   A surgeon put a leech on the end of a thumb she'd sewn back
    on. She said that research shows that using leeches increases the
    success rate of this kind of surgery.

    a   What sort of evidence might the researcher have collected?

    b   Suggest how this use of leeches works.

9   Dan had a blood clot in a vein in his leg.
    The consultant said that the clot could kill him if it moved to
    his heart or lungs. He gave him an injection of a substance from
    leech saliva.
    Describe how the injection helped.

10 Find out the name of the war in which doctors used antibiotics for
    the first time.
    (Hint: look back at Topic 8C.4.)

11 Some people don't want their wounds to be treated using maggots.
    Suggest why.

12 Working as a group, suggest some advantages and disadvantages of
    using maggots on infected wounds.

13 In your group, take another vote on whether you are willing to be
    treated using leeches and maggots.
    If anyone has changed their mind, find out why.

14 Scientists in the West reduced the amount of research on the use of
    phages to treat bacterial infections.
    Suggest why.

15 Suggest why scientists in the West are now looking again at the use
    of phages against bacteria.

8D.1 Classifying animals and plants

You should already know ⟩ Outcomes ⟩ Keywords ⟩

In this Unit, you will be looking at some adaptations of living things to the habitats in which they live.

When you study a **habitat**, you need to be able to identify the plants and animals that you find. It helps if you know which group they belong to. When we put plants and animals into groups, we say that we **classify** them.

Classifying animals

You have learned how we classify animals:

- animals with backbones are called **vertebrates**;
- animals without backbones are called **invertebrates**.

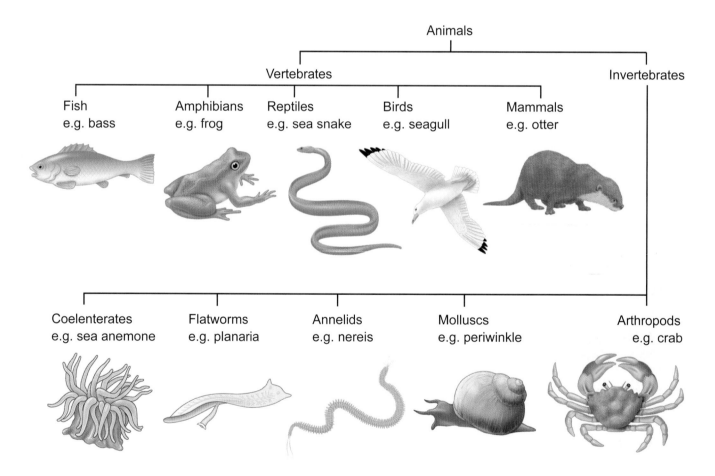

Animals

Vertebrates | Invertebrates

Fish
e.g. bass

Amphibians
e.g. frog

Reptiles
e.g. sea snake

Birds
e.g. seagull

Mammals
e.g. otter

Coelenterates
e.g. sea anemone

Flatworms
e.g. planaria

Annelids
e.g. nereis

Molluscs
e.g. periwinkle

Arthropods
e.g. crab

Question 1 2 3 4

Now let's classify green plants

There are hundreds of thousands of different green plants, so we divide them into smaller groups to help us to identify and study them.

There is more than one way of doing this.

Some plants have a special transport system for food and water called a vascular system. So we call these plants **vascular plants**.

Plants without a vascular system are called **non-vascular plants**.

Vascular and non-vascular plants are divided into smaller groups.

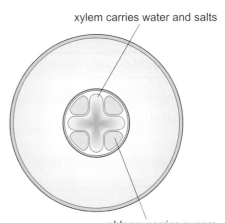

xylem carries water and salts

phloem carries sugars

A slice through the root of a vascular plant.

Question 5 6

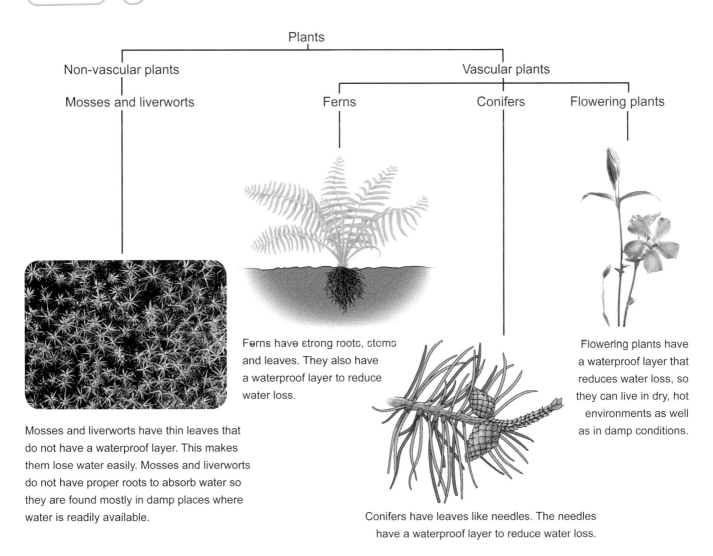

Ferns have strong roots, stems and leaves. They also have a waterproof layer to reduce water loss.

Flowering plants have a waterproof layer that reduces water loss, so they can live in dry, hot environments as well as in damp conditions.

Mosses and liverworts have thin leaves that do not have a waterproof layer. This makes them lose water easily. Mosses and liverworts do not have proper roots to absorb water so they are found mostly in damp places where water is readily available.

Conifers have leaves like needles. The needles have a waterproof layer to reduce water loss.

Question 7 8 9   Check your progress

You should already know | Outcomes | Keywords

Seasonal change

You have learned about some ways that animal behaviour changes with the seasons. Some animals hibernate and some migrate in order to survive. Migration and hibernation are linked to day length.

Breeding seasons

In animals that breed only at certain times of the year, breeding is linked to times when there is plenty of food. Many animals in the UK breed in the spring. External and internal factors affect when breeding starts.

When the day length is right for them to breed, animals make more **sex hormones**. These hormones stimulate **breeding behaviour** such as courting and nest building. These are innate behaviours, but animals become better at these things by trial and error. This is **learned behaviour**. Animals that have improved their courtship displays or have learned to build safer nests are the ones most likely to attract a mate.

> **Remember**
>
> The patterns of behaviour that newborn animals show are **innate**, or **instinctive**.
>
> For example, newborn babies will grip your finger and move their heads in search of a nipple. Later, they learn new behaviours.

Question 1 / 2 / 3 / 4

Tides affect when some marine animals breed. Some marine animals release eggs and sperm into the sea. To make sure that the eggs are fertilised, they all need to do it at the same time.

Horseshoe crabs come together in large groups to lay their eggs. Then there are more eggs and young at any one time than predators can eat.

Horseshoe crabs and turtles lay eggs in pits on sandy shores. Female turtles lay theirs above high-tide level. They leave the water at night during the highest tides. Tides are highest at the new moon and the full moon.

Male horseshoe crabs hold onto females and fertilise the eggs as they lay them.

Question 5 / 6

Breeding behaviour

To breed successfully in different situations, species develop different **behaviour patterns**. These include patterns of mating and parental care.

Gulls regurgitate fish to feed their young. When they are big enough, the young learn to fly and to find food.

The breeding behaviour of these two seagulls is very different.

Black headed gull

Kittiwake

Look at the table.

	Black-headed gull	Kittiwake
Nest	in colonies on the ground – a simple hollow	on small cliff ledges – use mud and seaweed to make a nest like a cup
Courting and mating	male displays to female and gives her food	male displays to female and gives her food
Alarm calls	often	rare
Mobbing predators	yes	no
Camouflaged young	yes	no
Feeding chicks on regurgitated food	parent has red bill young feed from bill	parent red inside mouth young feed from throat
When threatened by an adult	young run away	young stay still and hide their beaks

Question 7 8 9 10

Newly hatched young of geese and ducks are better developed. Their mothers protect them. They show them what to eat and where to find food, but the young feed themselves.

They leave the nest soon after hatching. They instinctively follow their mothers because they become **imprinted** on the first moving thing that they see. If what they see is not their mother, they may follow that instead. Birds of many species have become imprinted on humans. They behave as though humans are their species and don't try to mate with their own species.

Ducklings imprinted on Konrad Lorenz (1903–1989), who researched this behaviour.

Question 11 12 13

Collecting data to answer questions about a habitat

Molly and her class did some field work on a rocky shore. There are lots of plants and animals there. So this is an interesting place to study. Animals are harder to see in many other habitats.

The plants and animals found on the shore depend on each other. They are called a **community**.

Question 1 ───────────────

Asking questions before the visit

In the lesson before the visit, Molly's teacher asked the class to think about what they'd like to find out about the rocky shore. Molly and her friend came up with these ideas.

> What plants and animals live on the rocky shore?
>
> Will we find the same plants and animals on the same part of the shore?
>
> How can we find the numbers of the different plants and animals?
>
> Will different areas of the shore have different environmental conditions?

Question 2 ───────────────

It is often not possible to count all the individuals in a **population**, so we take a **sample**. Then we estimate the number of organisms that live in an area.

Question 3 ───────────────

It is easier to study the shore when the tide is out, but the seaweed makes it slippery.

When the tide comes in, it brings with it tiny floating plants and animals called plankton. Many shore animals feed on plankton.

Collecting the information

Molly decided to see whether different plants and animals lived on different parts of the shore.

Her teacher showed her how to use a **quadrat** to sample the shore life. She threw a plastic card on the ground and placed the quadrat so that the card was in the centre. Molly then wrote down the names of the different plants and animals in the quadrat.

She took ten samples near the top of the shore. She then moved nearer the sea and used the quadrat another ten times. Next, she used the quadrat another ten times near the sea.

Molly's teacher thought that this was a good idea. She asked David's group to do the same experiment so that they could compare the results when they got back to school.

Name	Quadrat number				
	1	2	3		
Periwinkle	III	II	₶		
Anemone	₶	III	I		
Barnacle	IIII	I			

Question 4

Looking at the results

When Molly looked at her results, she could see that different plants and animals lived on different areas of the shore.

Her teacher asked her to call the areas she sampled the upper, middle and lower shore. She explained that the habitats are different, and that different habitats support different living things. Look at the pictures.

The upper shore spends a lot of time out of the water. It is exposed to different weather conditions.

The middle shore spends less time under water than the lower shore. It is not exposed to the weather for as long as the upper shore.

The lower shore spends a lot of time under the water.

Question 5

From results to conclusions

Molly summarised her results in a table.

Area	Species found
Upper shore	Most of the rock is covered by black lichen. In rock crevices I found a few tiny periwinkles and barnacles.
Middle shore	I found lots of barnacles, limpets and mussels in this area of the shore. I also found some small pieces of seaweed in this area.
Lower shore	The seaweed was long and flexible. I could not remove it from the rock. I found crabs, starfish, limpets, fish and sea anemones here.

Question 6 / **7**

Explaining the differences

Back at school, the teacher asked the class to try to explain why there were different communities in different habitats. They thought that the **environmental conditions** were different in the different areas of the shore.

These are their ideas.

- **Upper shore**

  This area can dry out quickly because it spends a lot of the time not covered by the seawater. This means that there is less feeding time for the animals. It is often exposed to very hot or very cold weather conditions. Sometimes, rain makes the water less salty.

- **Middle shore**

  This area spends more time under water than the upper shore but less time under water than the lower shore. The water brings with it a rich supply of food.

- **Lower shore**

  This area spends most of the time under water. This means that there is less variation in temperature and not such a problem of drying.

Lichens are made of a green alga and a fungus. They often live on rocks and tree trunks. They can survive because they take a long time to dry out.

Question 8

Plants and animals on the shore have ways of making sure that the waves don't wash them away.

Many species of seaweed are long and flexible. They also have very strong holdfasts, which fix them to the rocks.

Limpet shells fit closely to the rock so that they don't dry out. They feed on tiny seaweeds on the rock when the tide is in.

Mussels live attached to rocks. They filter plankton from the water when the tide is in.

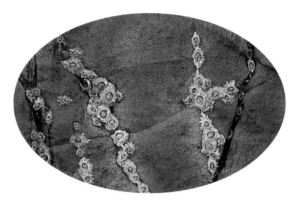

Barnacles are cemented to the rock. When the tide is in, they filter plankton from the water.

Question 9 / **10** / **11** ——————————

Population size and environmental conditions

Molly's teacher agreed with their ideas. She said that the size of the population of an organism is affected by environmental conditions such as the amounts of light, water and nutrients.

The teacher also said that organisms will have more chance of survival where there is less variation in temperature.

Molly looked at the results of her quadrats for the population of barnacles.

Area	Number of barnacles
Upper shore	5
Middle shore	62
Lower shore	0

Question 12 / **13** / **14** / **15** ——————————

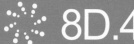

You should already know   Outcomes   Keywords

Food chains and webs

A **food chain** shows how energy is transferred from one organism to the next in a community. Each food chain starts with a green plant, which is called a **producer**.

An animal that feeds on green plants or other animals is called a **consumer**.

An animal that only eats plants is called a **herbivore**.

An animal that feeds on other animals is called a **carnivore**.

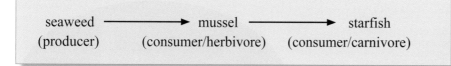

seaweed ⟶ mussel ⟶ starfish
(producer) (consumer/herbivore) (consumer/carnivore)

In most communities, plants and animals belong to more than one food chain. A number of food chains joined together is called a **food web**. This gives a more complete picture of how an animal feeds.

Here is part of a seashore food web.

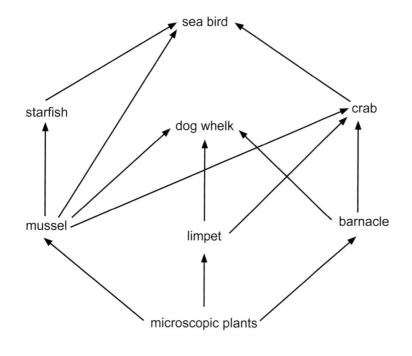

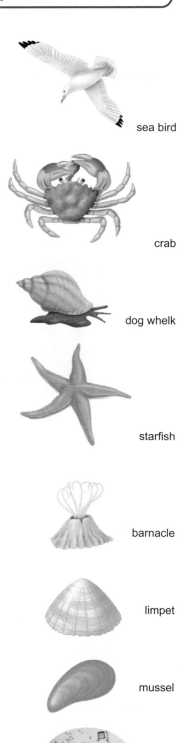

sea bird

crab

dog whelk

starfish

barnacle

limpet

mussel

microscopic plants

Question 1   2   3   4   5

Using food webs

We can use food webs to predict the effect of a rise or fall in the population size of a particular plant or animal in a community.

If the population of one organism goes up or down, it affects the rest of the food web.

If the mussels are killed by a disease:

- the number of limpets may also decrease – the dog whelks have fewer mussels to eat, so they eat more limpets;
- the number of sea birds may decrease because they have lost an important food source.

  Question 6 7

Pyramids of numbers

In a food chain, not all of the energy taken in by an organism passes to the next organism. Some is used for movement, growth and warmth. So there is less energy for the organisms at each stage in a food chain.

Because of this, the number of animals gets smaller as the food chain goes from stage to stage.

100 lettuces ⟶ 10 rabbits ⟶ 1 fox

We can show the change in population as we move along a food chain as a **pyramid of numbers**.

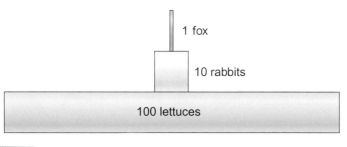

1 fox

10 rabbits

100 lettuces

Question 8

A problem with pyramids of number is that they do not allow for the size of the organism at each level of the food chain.

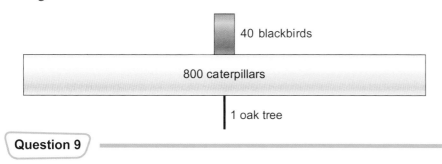

40 blackbirds

800 caterpillars

1 oak tree

Question 9

An oak tree is very big compared with a caterpillar. There is only one oak tree but it has thousands of leaves for caterpillars to feed on.

Review your work

Summary ➡

Types of investigation

You can gather evidence to answer a question in lots of different ways. You may have:

- done laboratory experiments like the investigation of woodlice;
- used secondary sources such as books or the Internet (information collected by other people is called **secondary data**);
- done field work, including doing surveys by sampling;
- done **surveys** of data about people, including people's opinions (these often involve questionnaires).

Question 1 **2** **3** **4**

Information

Scientific papers are the reports of their research that scientists publish in scientific journals. Martin searched for and downloaded papers from the Internet. These papers are secondary sources of information.

Question 5

While Martin studied the environment, Sally surveyed the opinions of people who lived or ran businesses in the area of the planned airport.

When people give their **opinions**, they say what they think.

- Often, they have no evidence for their ideas.
- Sometimes, these opinions are **biased**. They are conclusions that, if correct, would benefit them in some way.

An example is the case of the Little Owl.

Martin is researching the impact on the environment of a planned new airport. He is using scientific books and papers. We call this a desk study.

Martin uses traps to sample animals and **quadrats** to sample plants on the land where the airport is planned. This is field work.

Investigating the Little Owl

Just before the start of the 20th century, a few Little Owl pairs were introduced into Britain. By the 1930s, they were widespread and were being accused of killing wild birds and the chicks of game birds such as pheasants.

Gamekeepers killed Little Owls when they got the chance and wanted them to be wiped out entirely.

In 1935, the British Trust for Ornithology set up an enquiry to look for evidence of what the Little Owl actually ate. A naturalist called Alice Hibbert-Ware had already made observations of Little Owls and dissected their pellets. So the Trust asked her to find the answer.

Little Owls are predators.
In 1935, no one knew what they ate.

 Question 6 **7**

What Alice did

Experiment 1

Alice did experiments on captive owls to find out whether what was in the pellets matched what the owls had eaten. She found that it did.

Experiment 2

She analysed samples sent to her from dozens of places. These included 2460 pellets, 76 nest holes and 28 gizzards. (A gizzard is the part of a bird's stomach where food is ground up.)

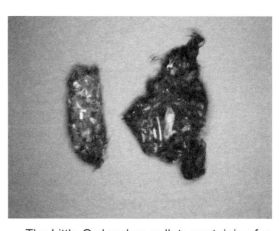

The Little Owl makes pellets containing fur, bones and other parts that it can't digest. It spits them out.

What Alice found in the pellets was a mixture of fur and bones of rodents, and the hard parts of insects and worms. She found the remains of birds in the nest hole of only one Little Owl.

She also considered other evidence: She looked at reports from:

- gamekeepers, about the loss of game birds to owls;
- landowners, who reported that their gamekeepers were saying that the shortage of pheasants was a result of Little Owls eating many of the chicks.

 Question 8 **9** **10** **11**

8D.1

1 What is the meaning of the word <u>habitat</u>?

2 a Name the <u>two</u> main groups of animals.

 b Which of the two groups has an inside skeleton?

3 a Write down the <u>five</u> groups of vertebrates.

 b For each group, write down <u>one</u> feature that makes it different from the other groups.

4 Name <u>five</u> groups of invertebrates.

5 Name <u>two</u> types of vascular tissue in vascular plants.

6 Why do we divide plants into groups?

7 Explain why mosses and liverworts often live in a damp environment.

8 Why can vascular plants live in a wide range of habitats?

9 Suggest <u>one</u> feature of the environment that conifers might be adapted to.

8D.2

1 a Write down <u>one</u> example of innate behaviour and one example of learned behaviour.

 b For each example, suggest how it helps the animal to survive.

2 Why is a good food supply important during the breeding season?

3 Sex hormones and day length affect breeding.
 Which of these is an external and which is an internal factor?

4 Describe <u>one</u> example of an instinctive behaviour being improved that benefits animals.

5 Describe <u>one</u> other example of an external factor affecting breeding season.

6 Horseshoe crabs come out of the water to breed mainly during high tides at night.
 Suggest <u>two</u> advantages of this timing.

7 Write down <u>three</u> things that might make a bird choose one mate rather than another.

8 Suggest how nesting in colonies (large groups), making alarm calls and mobbing predators help black-headed gulls survive.

continued

9 What innate feeding behaviour is the same for both of these gulls?

10 Young black-headed gulls run away from other gulls but young kittiwakes hide.
Suggest why they behave in different ways.

11 What do we call it when an animal recognises and follows another animal, usually its mother?

12 Explain why these ducklings are following Konrad Lorenz.

13 Suggest why imprinting is useful for survival of young.

8D.3

1 Write down one advantage and one problem of doing field work on a rocky shore.

2 Molly's friend David said, 'We can just count all the plants and animals that we see.'
Explain why this is not a good idea.

3 Write down two safety points that the class needs to think about before working on the rocky shore.

4 Why was it a good idea for several groups to do the same experiment?

5 Which of these areas is covered by the sea for the longest time?

6 What patterns can you see in Molly's data?

7 Molly's friend Patrick suggested that it would be a good idea to take some of the limpets back to the laboratory to look at in more detail. Why must they not do this?

8 Lichens take a long time to dry out.
Why is this useful for an organism that lives on the upper shore?

9 Explain why seaweeds have strong holdfasts.

10 Mussels, limpets and barnacles fasten themselves to rocks in different ways.

   a Find out how each attaches itself to the rock.

   b How does attachment to rock help these animals to survive?

11 Barnacles and mussels keep their shells tightly shut until the tide comes in.
Suggest two reasons for this.

12 Which area of the shore contained the largest population of barnacles?

continued

13 Molly said, 'More barnacles live on the middle shore than the upper shore because the barnacles on the middle shore have more time to feed from the water.'

Do you agree or disagree with Molly's conclusion? Explain your answer.

14 Molly made the conclusion just from looking at her own results. If she is a good scientist, what should she do to make sure that the conclusion is correct?

15 Explain <u>one</u> other factor that makes it easier for barnacles to survive on the middle shore than the upper shore.

8D.4

1 From the food web, write down:

a the producer;

b <u>one</u> consumer.

2 Use the food web to find <u>two</u> things that crabs eat.

3 Write down <u>two</u> food chains in the food web that end with a sea bird.

4 Name <u>one</u> herbivore in the food web.

5 Name <u>one</u> carnivore in the food web.

6 What will happen to the crab population if all the mussels are killed?

7 Limpets feed on microscopic plants on the rocks. What effect will an oil spill on the rocks have on the food web? Explain your answer.

8 Draw the shape of the pyramid of numbers for each of these food chains.

a dandelions ⟶ rabbits ⟶ fox

b microscopic plants ⟶ insect larvae ⟶ perch ⟶ pike

9 Draw a pyramid of numbers for each of these food chains.

a 100 lettuces ⟶ 10 000 slugs ⟶ 100 thrushes ⟶ 1 hawk

b 1 rose bush ⟶ 10 000 greenfly ⟶ 1000 ladybirds

8D.HSW

1   What is secondary data?

2   List some secondary sources of information about life in a pond.

3   Look at the pictures. Martin is using several different methods to investigate the likely effect of a new airport on the environment. Describe the kind of investigation that each picture shows.

4   Suggest the subjects of <u>two</u> kinds of scientific report that Martin probably looked for.

5   Martin didn't just use his computer for finding information.
    Work as a group to think of the ways that Martin might use his computer in his investigation.

6   What did gamekeepers say about the Little Owl?

7   What is an owl pellet?

8   Little Owl was on trial. What sort of evidence was needed to prove whether it was guilty or innocent? Hint: look at the pictures.

9   Read about the Little Owl and find an example of each of the following.

    a   Hearsay – when one person reports what another person said. Courts don't accept hearsay. It is not evidence.

    b   A biased opinion – when a particular idea is useful to someone.

    c   Valid evidence.

10 A possible conclusion about the information sent in by the gamekeepers and landowners was that it consisted of biased opinions.
    Why might these people want to believe that the Little Owl preyed on game birds?

11 The evidence from the pellets and the reports from the gamekeepers didn't match.
    What was it about Alice's work that made the British Trust for Ornithology accept her conclusions that the Little Owl was not a pest, but was a useful bird?

The photograph shows a wooden pepper mill. Wood is the **material** the mill is made from. A material is not the same as an object.

Think about a plastic ruler. The ruler is an <u>object</u>, it is made out of plastic. Plastic is the <u>material</u>.

Some materials are made out of combinations of other materials. Concrete is made from sand, cement and small stones. We know that concrete contains sand, but sand itself is made from other things, even though it does not look like it is.

After thousands of years and many mistakes, scientists finally worked out that all materials are made from just a few substances.

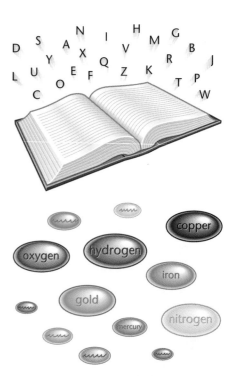

Wood is the <u>material</u> that makes up this pepper mill. The pepper mill is an <u>object</u>. Wood is a natural material.

Question 1 **2**

What is an element?

Substances are made up of <u>particles</u>.

Some substances are made from only one type of particle. They are not combinations of other substances in any way. They are <u>pure</u> substances. They are called **elements**.

Elements combine together to make other substances. This is like the letters in the alphabet. There are about 750 000 English words, but they are all made from 26 letters.

There are about 100 elements. Any material that is not an element is made up from some combination of the elements.

Examples of elements include oxygen, hydrogen, copper, gold, iron, nitrogen and mercury. Materials like wood, water, ink, paper, calcium carbonate and hydrochloric acid are made from combinations of elements.

For years, people tried to find the elements that made gold. Unfortunately, gold is an element – you cannot make it from something else!

There are about 100 elements that make millions of substances, just like letters make words.

Question 3 **4**

About elements

You can see that some things are not elements just by looking. If you look at concrete under a microscope, you can see that it is made of pieces of sand and different coloured crystals. It cannot be an element if it is made from more than one thing.

Wood is another material that you can tell is not an element just by looking.

 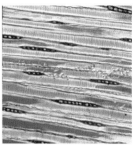

Concrete under a microscope.

Wood under a microscope.

More often, you cannot tell just by looking whether something is an element. Water looks like it is not made from anything else but it is not an element. People believed that water was an element until 1800, when someone passed an electric current through water. The water split up into hydrogen and oxygen, the two elements that it is made from.

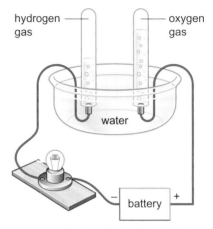

Electricity splits water into its elements.

Question 5 **6**

Some elements, like gold and copper, have been known since ancient times. Others, like radium, have only been discovered in the past hundred years or so.

The chart shows how common different elements are in the Earth's surface. If gold was as common as aluminium, it would probably not be worth as much!

Of the hundred or so elements, about 80 are metals. At room temperature, most of the metals are solid. An exception to this is mercury, which is a liquid at room temperature. Mercury freezes into a solid about 39 °C below the freezing point of water.

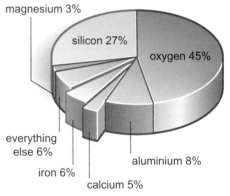

Pie chart showing how much of these elements there is in the Earth's crust.

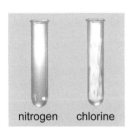 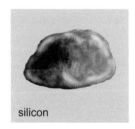 

nitrogen chlorine   silicon   gold

carbon   iodine   mercury   sodium   sulfur

All of these are elements.

Question 7

What are atoms?

Over 2000 years ago a Greek philosopher called Democritus suggested that everything was made of small **particles**, which he called 'atoms'. Atoms are too small to see, even with a microscope. The particles that make up matter are single atoms or groups of atoms joined together.

The way the particles in a material are arranged makes a particular material a solid, a liquid or a gas.

You cannot see atoms using a microscope but you can find out things about them using X-rays and other methods. You can also detect atoms in other ways. If you polish a piece of aluminium with a cloth, you will be able to smell the metal because some aluminium particles have gone into the air and into your nose.

You can smell the aluminium. This is evidence for the existence of aluminium atoms.

This coin from the time of Elizabeth the First is made from silver atoms.

If you look at it under a microscope, the atoms are too small to see.

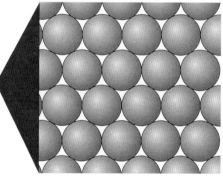

If we could see the silver atoms, they would look something like this.

Question 1 **2**

An **element** is a substance made from just one type of atom. Gold contains only gold atoms and silver contains only silver atoms. So gold and silver are both elements.

Water contains hydrogen and oxygen atoms. Water is not an element – it is made up from the elements hydrogen and oxygen. We say that water is a **compound**, because it is made of more than one element joined together.

Substance	What is in it
carbon dioxide	carbon, oxygen
limestone	calcium, carbon, oxygen
salt	sodium, chlorine
iron	iron

Question 3 **4**

Symbols

The different elements have their own **symbols**. All the symbols begin with a capital letter. Some symbols have a second letter in small case. No symbol has three letters. The table shows the symbols and gives some other information for some common elements.

Name	Symbol	Metal or non-metal?	Solid, liquid or gas at 20 °C?	Colour	Year discovered
bromine	Br	non-metal	liquid	brown	1826
calcium	Ca	metal	solid	grey	1808
carbon	C	non-metal	solid	black	ancient
chlorine	Cl	non-metal	gas	green	1810
copper	Cu	metal	solid	pink	ancient
gold	Au	metal	solid	gold	ancient
helium	He	non-metal	gas	colourless	1868
hydrogen	H	non-metal	gas	colourless	1783
iron	Fe	metal	solid	grey	ancient
magnesium	Mg	metal	solid	grey	1808
mercury	Hg	metal	liquid	silver	ancient
nitrogen	N	non-metal	gas	colourless	1772
oxygen	O	non-metal	gas	colourless	1774
silver	Ag	metal	solid	silver	ancient
sulfur	S	non-metal	solid	yellow	ancient

Scientists use the symbol to represent one atom of an element. 'Cu' means 'one atom of copper'. 'Fe' means 'one atom of iron'.

Molecules

A **molecule** is the particle you get when two or more atoms join together. Molecules can be very big. Some molecules contain hundreds of atoms.

The particles of carbon dioxide are molecules. Each molecule is made of one carbon atom and two oxygen atoms stuck together.

In the gas oxygen, the atoms go round in pairs. A molecule of oxygen is made from two oxygen atoms stuck together.

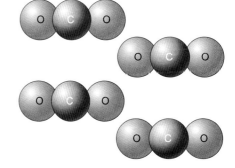

A model of carbon dioxide molecules.

Question 5 6 7

Check your progress

8E.3 Changes

You should already know

Outcomes

Keywords

There are two types of change. One type does not make any new substances. This is called a **physical change**. Examples of physical changes include melting, boiling, and breaking a sheet of glass. After a physical change, the substance might look very different but it is still the same substance. The atoms might end up in different places but the way they form arrangements with other atoms is not changed.

The second type of change is called a **chemical change**. In a chemical change, new substances are formed because atoms change places and combine with each other in new ways. Burning is an example of a chemical change. When a substance burns, its atoms combine with oxygen atoms from the air. The ashes are a new substance. They are some sort of oxide – the precise sort depends upon what was burned. Other common examples of chemical changes are:

- food being cooked;
- food being digested;
- iron rusting;
- leaves rotting.

Question 1 2 3

Substances made from different atoms joined together are not elements because they contain more than one type of atom. We call them **compounds**. Most of the substances we use are compounds. The table shows a few examples.

Compound	Atoms in it	Some uses
water	hydrogen, oxygen	cooking, drinking, washing
common salt	sodium, chlorine	cooking, melting ice
carbon dioxide	carbon, oxygen	fizzy drinks, fire extinguishers

Question 4

Water looks different from ice but they are the same substance.

Burning is an irreversible chemical change.

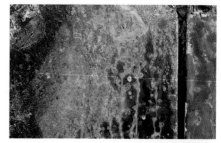

Rusty iron.

Using salt to help thaw ice on roads.

New materials

We use chemical changes on a large scale to make useful substances like iron. Iron is made from iron ore, which is found in the ground. Iron ore contains the compound iron oxide. This is made from iron atoms and oxygen atoms combined.

A chemical change is needed to separate the iron from the oxygen. This is done in a <u>blast furnace</u>. Carbon, oxygen and limestone are heated to a very high temperature to make a chemical change happen. One of the new materials produced is iron metal. The blast furnace is so hot that liquid iron collects in the bottom of the furnace.

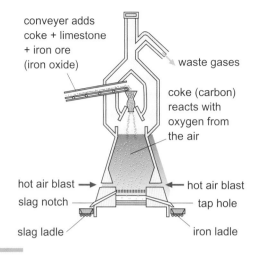

Making iron in a blast furnace.

Question 5

The <u>properties</u> of a substance are the things that we can see and measure about it, including the things it does. The new materials made in a chemical change have different properties from the substances they are made from.

Burning magnesium is a good example of a chemical change.

Magnesium is an element. Its properties include the following:

- it is a soft, shiny metal at room temperature;
- it will conduct electricity;
- it can be bent and smoothed out into flexible strips;
- its melting point is 651 °C.

Oxygen is an element. Its properties include:

- it is a colourless gas at room temperature;
- it has no smell;
- it does not conduct electricity;
- its melting point is −214 °C.

When magnesium burns, the word equation for the reaction is:

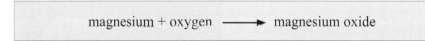

$$\text{magnesium} + \text{oxygen} \longrightarrow \text{magnesium oxide}$$

The product, magnesium oxide, is a compound. Its properties include:

- it is a white powdery solid at room temperature;
- it does not conduct electricity unless you melt it;
- its melting point is 2800 °C.

The product bears no resemblance to the reactants.

Question 6 **7**

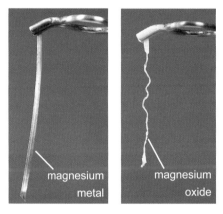

When the magnesium burns,
it reacts with oxygen from the air.

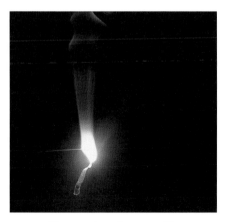

Magnesium burns with a very
bright, white flame.

You should already know | Outcomes | Keywords

Patterns in the elements

There are about 100 different elements. Over the centuries, many different scientists have studied elements, trying to predict what they do in reactions.

After a lot of work by a lot of people, a very useful chart of the elements was put together. It is called the **periodic table**.

This periodic table shows the position of the elements in the table with their symbol and name.

Remember
Every element has a symbol made up from one or two letters.

Group 1	2											Group 3	4	5	6	7	Group 0
				H hydrogen													He helium
Li lithium	Be beryllium											B boron	C carbon	N nitrogen	O oxygen	F fluorine	Ne neon
Na sodium	Mg magnesium											Al aluminium	Si silicon	P phosphorus	S sulfur	Cl chlorine	Ar argon
K potassium	Ca calcium	Sc scandium	Ti titanium	V vanadium	Cr chromium	Mn manganese	Fe iron	Co cobalt	Ni nickel	Cu copper	Zn zinc	Ga gallium	Ge germanium	As arsenic	Se selenium	Br bromine	Kr krypton
Rb rubidium	Sr strontium	Y yttrium	Zr zirconium	Nb niobium	Mo molybdenum	Tc technetium	Ru ruthenium	Rh rhodium	Pd palladium	Ag silver	Cd cadmium	In indium	Sn tin	Sb antimony	Te tellurium	I iodine	Xe xenon
Cs caesium	Ba barium	elements 57–71	Hf hafnium	Ta tantalum	W tungsten	Re rhenium	Os osmium	Ir iridium	Pt platinum	Au gold	Hg mercury	Tl thallium	Pb lead	Bi bismuth	Po polonium	At astatine	Rn radon
Fr francium	Ra radium	elements 89+															

Elements in the periodic table.

The first thing to remember about the periodic table is that the columns with numbers are called **groups**. Elements in the same group have similar **properties**.

For example, lithium, sodium and potassium are in Group 1. They are all soft metals that react very dangerously with water.

a Lithium. **b** Sodium. **c** Potassium.

Question 1 | 2 | 3

Group 0

This group is on the extreme right of the periodic table. It contains six elements. They are sometimes called the <u>noble gases</u>. The table gives some information about the first three.

Name	Symbol	Information
helium	He	Colourless gas. Does not react with any other element. Used in aqualungs for divers.
neon	Ne	Colourless gas. Does not react with any other element. Used in electric advertising signs because it produces a red glow.
argon	Ar	Colourless gas. Does not react with any other element. Used in light bulbs so that the hot wire does not burn.

Question 4 5

Non-metals are on the right

The chart shows a simple extract from the periodic table with illustrations of some elements. The elements in the blue area of the table are all metals. The elements in the pale brown area on the right-hand side are non-metals. You can carry the zigzag division down the full table to divide the metals from the non-metals.

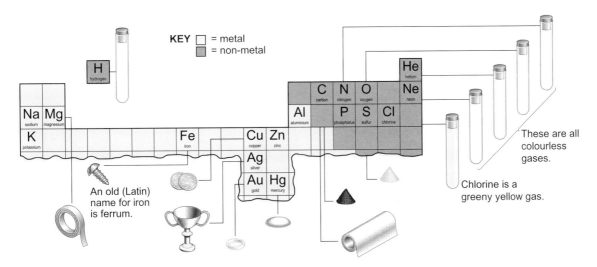

KEY ☐ = metal   ■ = non-metal

These are all colourless gases.

Chlorine is a greeny yellow gas.

An old (Latin) name for iron is ferrum.

The study of the periodic table is a massive subject. When scientists understand the information in it, they can make predictions about how elements will behave in reactions. They can also make good guesses about the properties of elements they have never even seen!

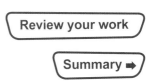

Review your work

Summary ➡

Question 6 7

You should already know

Outcomes

Keywords

Collaboration

The periodic table of the elements was the result of the work of many scientists over many years. This is an example of people sharing work and ideas with others. We call this **collaboration**.

What scientists knew by 1860

By 1860, scientists already knew some important things as a result of many years' work by many different people. They knew:

- that everything is made from a few substance called elements;
- that elements are made up from one type of atom;
- that some elements behave in similar ways; for example, calcium and magnesium both burn brightly, and produce an oxide that dissolves in water to make an alkali.

In 1860, the world's first chemistry conference took place at Karlsruhe in Germany. Scientists from all over the world attended it. This was a chance for collaboration. At the conference, the scientists published an up-to-date list of how heavy the atoms of different elements were. This led to the discovery of the periodic table of the elements. The discovery happened because some scientists who were at the conference used the new information on how heavy the atoms of different elements were.

Newlands' discovery

1n 1864, a scientist called John Newlands wrote down a list of the elements he knew in the order of how heavy they were. He noticed that, if you counted seven along from any element, you came to an element with similar properties. If you write the elements out in rows, elements that behave in a similar way appear underneath each other.

Newlands' discovery was interesting, but there was a problem. The patterns only worked for the first 20 elements.

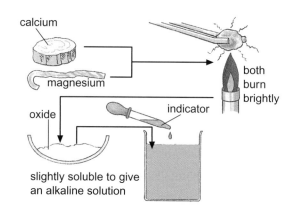

Calcium and magnesium behave in similar ways.

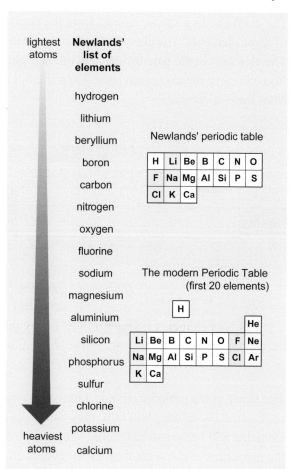

Question 1   2

Improving on the idea

A Russian scientist called Dmitri Mendeleev not only improved on the idea, he also used it to make **predictions** that could be tested.

To do this Mendeleev had to overcome some problems.

* At the time, only about 60 elements had been discovered.
* Some of the information people thought they knew was wrong, including how heavy the atoms were.

He found a way round the problems by leaving spaces in his table where the properties of an element did not fit. He also swapped the order of elements round where he thought the data on how heavy the atoms were was wrong. Two elements he did this with were tellurium and iodine. The properties of iodine made it so like fluorine, chlorine and bromine that it made sense to put it in the same column. Mendeleev was being **critical** of the evidence from experiments here. He sometimes let his ideas of a pattern in the table override the experimental result, because he thought that the experimental result must be wrong.

Mendeleev ended up with a table with quite a few holes in it. Then he did a brave thing. He predicted what the missing elements would be like from what he knew of the others near them in the table. These predictions could be put to the test by other scientists. Three of the elements Mendeleev predicted were discovered by other scientists within 15 years. Mendeleev was right!

The missing group

One thing that Mendeleev did not predict was a whole group of elements! Four of the noble gases – argon, neon, krypton and xenon – were discovered by a Scot called William Ramsay. He worked out that all these elements fitted in the periodic table as another group. The discovery came from a **conflict** of evidence. The mass of nitrogen made from the air was slightly different from the mass of nitrogen made in other ways. Ramsay worked out that the nitrogen made from the air contained a small amount of argon.

Another problem

If you put the elements in order of how heavy they are, some of the elements do not fit into pattern of the periodic table. Argon is an example. It fits before potassium but it is heavier. This conflict eventually produced a new idea. In 1913, a scientist called Henry Moseley worked out that the table should be put in an order based on how the atoms in elements were made up. This was a better idea than using mass and gives us the table we use today.

  Question 3   4

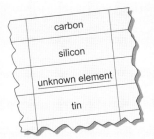

What Mendeleev said the unknown element would be like (in 1869)
* a grey metal
* its oxide would be white
* its chloride:
    would boil at less than 100°C
    each cm³ would have mass 1.9 g

The element germanium (discovered 27 years later)
* a grey metal
* a white oxide
* its chloride:
    boils at 86.5°C
    each cm³ has mass 1.8 g

Sir William Ramsay won a Nobel Prize for discovering the missing group in the periodic table.

Group							0
1	2	3	4	5	6	7	He
Li	Be	B	C	N	O	F	Ne
Na	Mg	Al	Si	P	S	Cl	Ar
K	Ca						

(H is shown above the table; relative atomic masses: argon (Ar) = 40, potassium (K) = 39)

Argon is heavier than potassium but it fits in the pattern before it.

8E.1

1   What material is each of these items made from?

   a   A paper cup.

   b   A wooden chair.

   c   A steel blade.

   d   A cotton shirt.

2   Some things are made from more than one material. For example, a pencil is made from wood and graphite.

   Give two other examples of items made from several materials.

3   a   What are elements?

   b   Give five examples of elements.

4   The alchemists in the Middle Ages tried to find ways of changing lead (which was cheap) into gold (which was valuable).

   a   Why was this never going to work?

   b   Suggest why the alchemists kept trying to do this.

5   List three everyday substances that you can tell are not elements just by looking.
   Give a reason for each answer.

6   Why is water not an element?
   What is it made from?

7   Find out who discovered radium and why radium is a very dangerous element.

8E.2

1   What are atoms?

2   Although the idea of atoms has been around for a long time, it was only accepted as true by many people in the past hundred years or so.
   Why do you think that is the case?

3   What is the name for a substance made from more than one type of atom?

4   Copy out the table and add a third column classifying each substance as an element or a compound.

5   What do most of the non-metals in the table have in common and which two are the exceptions?

6   Find out why the symbol for iron is Fe and not something more obvious like Ir.

7   Using the diagram of carbon dioxide molecules as a guide, draw your own suggestion for a diagram of an oxygen molecule.

8E.3

1   What is the difference between a physical change and a chemical change?

2   What is produced in a chemical change?
   Why does this happen?

continued

3 Give <u>two</u> examples of chemical changes. For each, describe how you can tell that a new substance has been produced.

4 Give <u>three</u> examples of common compounds and list the elements that make them up.

5 **a** Describe how iron is made from iron ore.

b Many scientists would say that elements cannot be made from any other substance. How can that be true if iron is an element and it can be made from iron ore?

6 What reaction takes place when magnesium burns? Name the reactants and the product.

7 **a** How do you know that a chemical reaction has taken place when magnesium burns?

b Give <u>three</u> examples of the properties of the product that tell you it is a new substance.

8E.4

1 What is the periodic table and what type of information does it show?

2 What is the name for the columns with numbers at the top, and what is special about elements in the same column?

3 Suggest <u>one</u> reason why lithium, sodium and potassium all fit well in the same group.

4 In the English language, the term 'noble' can mean someone who is a knight, lord or lady, or is related in some way to the Royal Family. Until recently, it would have been very unusual for a 'noble' to associate with common people.

Why do you think the gases in Group 0 became known as 'noble gases'?

5 Suggest <u>one</u> reason why a gas that does not react is useful in a light bulb.

6 Give <u>one</u> difference between carbon and aluminium that you can tell from their positions in the periodic table. Give a reason for your answer.

7 Name an element that has similar properties to sodium. Give a reason for your answer.

8E.HSW

1 The elements sodium, potassium and lithium are all in the same group in the periodic table.

Find out what properties they have in common that someone like John Newlands might have known about.

2 Why was the chemistry conference in 1860 an example of collaboration between scientists?

3 **a** Find out some key facts about Mendeleev.

b There is a memorial to him in the periodic table itself. What is it?

4 Find out what honour William Ramsay received for his work on the periodic table and what tragedy occurred to prevent Henry Moseley producing more important ideas.

You should already know

Outcomes

Keywords

What's in a name?

A **compound** has a **chemical name**, like carbon dioxide or sodium chloride.

Compounds that we use in everyday life often have a common name that we use most of the time, like 'salt'. The chemical name sometimes gives you a clue about what is in the compound. For example, carbon dioxide contains carbon and oxygen, and copper oxide contains copper and oxygen. Sometimes, the chemical name is not as good at telling you what is in the compound.

'Pass the sodium chloride, please.'

The other thing to remember is that we sometimes get the same compound in forms that look quite different, probably with different common names. This can be for a range of reasons.

- The different substances might be made from crystals or grains of different sizes.
- The different substances might be mixed with different impurities.
- The way the atoms or molecules are arranged in the substance can make it look different even though the atoms inside the substances are the same. Graphite and diamond are both pure carbon but they have very different properties because of the way the carbon atoms are arranged.

Carbon (diamond).

When a substance melts or evaporates, it changes its appearance. Sometimes its name changes as well. For example, ice, water and steam are all the same compound.

The table gives some more examples.

Common name	Chemical name	Elements inside it
salt	sodium chloride	sodium, chlorine
chalk	calcium carbonate	calcium, carbon, oxygen
limestone	calcium carbonate	calcium, carbon, oxygen
natural gas	methane	carbon, hydrogen
alcohol	ethanol	carbon, hydrogen, oxygen

Carbon (graphite).

Question 1   2

What is a formula?

Scientist use a **formula** for each compound to show exactly what atoms are in each particle of the compound. The name might vary from one country to another but the formula is the same in any language. Formulae are made up from the symbols for the elements in a compound.

Water is H_2O everywhere in the world.

- The symbol for an atom on its own means there is one of those atoms in a particle of the substance. Hydrochloric acid has the formula HCl. 'H' means 'one atom of hydrogen'. 'Cl' means 'one atom of chlorine'.

- If there are two or more atoms in the particle then the number of them is written below the line after the symbol. Carbon dioxide has the formula CO_2. 'C' means 'one atom of carbon'. 'O_2' means 'two atoms of oxygen'.

Here are some examples.

Carbon dioxide.

Chemical name	Formula	What each particle contains
calcium oxide	CaO	one calcium atom, one oxygen atom
magnesium sulfide	MgS	one magnesium atom, one sulfur atom
carbon dioxide	CO_2	one carbon atom, two oxygen atoms
calcium carbonate	$CaCO_3$	one calcium atom, one carbon atom, three oxygen atoms

 **Question 3** **4**

In science, the plural of formula is usually <u>formulae</u> not formulas. A reaction can be described in words or with a formula.

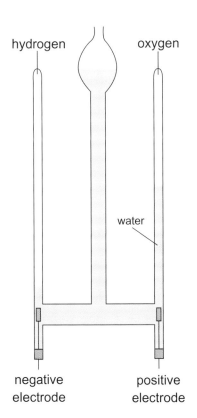

Words	hydrogen + chlorine $\longrightarrow$ hydrogen chloride
Formula	H_2 + Cl_2 $\longrightarrow$ 2HCl

These descriptions are both types of **equation**.

The first equation is a **word equation**. It tells you the names of the reactants and the products in the reaction.

The second equation is called a **chemical equation**. It shows how the atoms in the reactants change places to make the products. In this case, a molecule made of two hydrogen atoms reacts with a molecule made from two chlorine atoms. The product is two molecules of hydrogen joined to chlorine, called hydrogen chloride.

Both types of equation should be written on one line.

> **Remember**
>
> <u>Reactants</u> are the substances at the start of a reaction.
>
> <u>Products</u> are the substances that the reaction produces.

 Question 5   **6**

| You should already know | Outcomes | Keywords |

Products are different from reactants

Sodium chloride is a compound made from the elements sodium and chlorine.

When these two elements meet, they react violently to produce white crystals of sodium chloride. It is a new substance made from two different elements, so it is a compound.

We know that the reaction is a chemical reaction because salt is a new substance. It is very different from both sodium and chlorine.

Compounds are always different from the elements they are made from.

The product, salt, is safe enough to eat provided that you do not eat more than about 6 g a day.

Sodium is a reactive metal that will react violently with water to produce hydrogen.

Chlorine is a pale green gas that is very poisonous.

Sodium chloride is the salt that we add to our food to give it a salty taste.

Iron sulfide is a compound made from iron and sulfur. Not only does it look very different, but it is also not magnetic like iron even though half its atoms are iron.

The word equation for the reaction between iron and sulfur is:

$$\text{iron} + \text{sulfur} \longrightarrow \text{iron sulfide}$$

iron   +   sulfur

iron sulfide

Elements and compounds react to produce new substances in chemical reactions. Sometimes it can be quite difficult to tell whether a new substance has been produced. For example, you do not always notice a gas being produced. There are some things that provide clues to tell us whether a chemical reaction has happened. Remember, these are only clues. Sometimes they can be misleading!

- A gas is produced.
- The colour changes.
- Heat is produced.
- There is a change in mass.
- There is a change in appearance.

Question 1 / 2

Compounds and some of their reactions

Some compounds are very reactive. However, some compounds are less reactive and will only react under certain conditions.

Scientists use terms to describe different types of reactions.

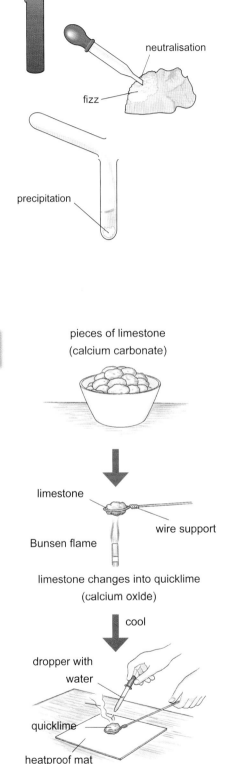

burning

neutralisation

fizz

precipitation

- Words used to describe reactions with oxygen include burning, **combustion**, oxidation and even respiration.
- When an acid reacts with an alkali, the properties of the acid and alkali are cancelled out. These are **neutralisation** reactions.
- In some reactions between two solutions, one of the products is insoluble and settles as a solid called a precipitate. These are called **precipitation** reactions.
- Some compounds break down or decompose when you heat them. This is called **thermal decomposition**. For example, potassium nitrate has the formula KNO_3. If you heat it, it melts at $334\,°C$ and decomposes at $400\,°C$. Oxygen gas is given off.

Another good example of thermal decomposition happens when you heat limestone to about $550\,°C$. The chemical name for limestone is calcium carbonate. The word equation for the reaction is:

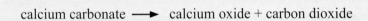

calcium carbonate ⟶ calcium oxide + carbon dioxide

Calcium carbonate and calcium oxide look very similar. They behave in very different ways.

- If you drip water onto calcium carbonate, nothing happens.
- If you drip water onto calcium oxide, you get a reaction that produces a lot of heat, and so the water turns to steam.

The common name for calcium oxide is quicklime.

Calcium oxide is a compound of calcium and oxygen. Its formula is CaO.

The chemical equation for the thermal decomposition reaction that makes it is:

$$CaCO_3 \longrightarrow CaO + CO_2$$

Quicklime is a very useful substance. People have been making it on a large scale in lime kilns since Roman times.

pieces of limestone
(calcium carbonate)

limestone

wire support

Bunsen flame

limestone changes into quicklime
(calcium oxide)

cool

dropper with
water

quicklime

heatproof mat

Question 3 4 5 6

Check your progress

You should already know

Outcomes

Keywords

What is a mixture?

A pure element is made up of identical particles. All the atoms in it are the same.

A pure compound is made up of identical particles, but each particle contains more than one different type of atom joined together.

A **mixture** is not pure. A mixture contains more than one substance. It contains more than one type of particle. The particles are not joined together. A mixture is made of different particles just mixed together. Seawater, air and tea are all examples of mixtures.

Look at the particle diagrams.

The first diagram shows hydrogen molecules. It is not a mixture. There is only one substance present. It is an element because everything is made from the same atom, hydrogen.

The second diagram shows the compound water. It is not an element because it is made of hydrogen and oxygen atoms. It is not a mixture because there are only water molecules in it.

The third diagram shows a mixture of different gases. The table below gives the formulae and names for four of the gases in the diagram.

Formula	Description
O_2	two oxygen atoms joined make an oxygen molecule
H_2	two hydrogen atoms joined make a hydrogen molecule
NH_3	one nitrogen atom joined to three hydrogen atoms make a molecule of ammonia
N_2	two nitrogen atoms joined make a molecule of nitrogen

Question 1 2

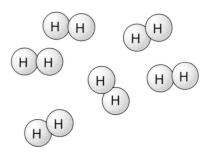
A particle diagram of a pure element.

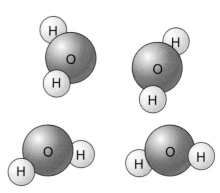
A particle diagram of a pure compound.

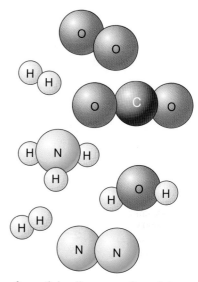
A particle diagram of a mixture.

Mineral water is a mixture

There are many examples of mixtures. For example, mineral water is a mixture. Look at the label.

The different minerals listed on the label have dissolved in the water during its journey from rainwater to mineral water. It has passed over and through many different rocks. The minerals in the water have come from reactions with those rocks and because some minerals in the rocks are soluble in water. When you dissolve something in water, you get a mixture.

One litre of the water shown in the chart has almost half a gram of solids dissolved in it. If that water is evaporated or boiled away in a kettle or pipe, the solids are left behind and they clog up the kettle or pipe. This is called <u>scale</u>.

Typical analysis mg/l	
Calcium	60
Magnesium	15
Sodium	46
Potassium	2.2
Carbonate ($CaCO_3$)	145
Chloride	155
Sulfate	1
Nitrate	5
Fluoride	0.1
Total dissolved solids	**453**

Question 3

Seawater is a mixture

Seawater is also a mixture. It contains many different solids, called salts, dissolved in the water. There is an average of 40 g of salts dissolved in every kilogram of water from an ocean.

The Dead Sea is not really a sea. It is a very large lake on the border between Jordon and Israel. The River Jordan flows into the Dead Sea but there is no outlet.

There are about 370 g of salts dissolved in every kilogram of water from the Dead Sea. The Dead Sea is the world's saltiest natural lake. It is one of the greatest sources of minerals in the world. Over 43 billion tonnes of salts are dissolved in the Dead Sea, of which almost 2 billion tonnes are potassium chloride.

The water going into the Dead Sea is not particularly salty. However, the local climate is extremely hot and dry, so the rate of evaporation of water is high. Water evaporates and leaves the salts behind. The Dead Sea is a bit like a huge evaporating dish.

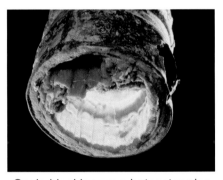

Scale blocking up a hot water pipe.

The water in the Dead Sea contains so much dissolved salt that you can easily float in it.

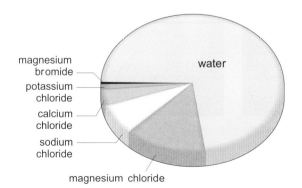

Mineral	% mass
magnesium chloride	14.5
sodium chloride	7.5
calcium chloride	3.8
potassium chloride	1.2
magnesium bromide	0.5
water	72.5

Mineral	Amount (billion tonnes)
magnesium chloride	22
sodium chloride	12
calcium chloride	6
potassium chloride	2
magnesium bromide	1

Salts in the Dead Sea.

Question 4   **5**

| You should already know | Outcomes | Keywords |

Air is a special mixture

The air is not a single substance. It is a mixture of several important gases.

Gas	Percentage in air
oxygen	21
nitrogen	78
argon (and other noble gases)	1
carbon dioxide	0.035
water	6 – 0.1

The table shows the composition of the mixture we call air and lists some important points about the gases that make it up.

The gases in the air.

Gas	Properties
Oxygen	Living things need this gas for their life processes.
Nitrogen	Nitrogen is unreactive. It is used to store food and materials that can be spoiled by reacting with oxygen.
Argon	Argon is a noble gas – it does not react with anything. It is used in light bulbs because it will not react with the hot filament.
Carbon dioxide	Carbon dioxide is a heavy gas. It can be used to keep oxygen off something. It is used in fire extinguishers, fizzy drinks and to store frozen food.
Water vapour	The amount of water vapour in the air varies depending on the weather. It can be between 0.1% and 6.0%.

In hospital, patients with breathing or heart problems are sometimes given pure oxygen to breathe rather than air. This makes it easier for them to absorb oxygen into their blood.

Argon won't react with the metal filament in a light bulb, even when it is white hot.

Question 1 2 3

Separating the air

Because air is a mixture, it can be separated without using a chemical reaction. This is done by cooling the air mixture down.

The chart shows the temperatures at which the gases change from a gas to either a liquid or a solid.

Temperature	What happens
0 °C	water vapour freezes
−79 °C	carbon dioxide gas changes into a solid – this is often called 'dry ice'
−183 °C	oxygen condenses into a liquid
−186 °C	argon condenses into a liquid
−196 °C	nitrogen condenses into a liquid

Liquid nitrogen.

Liquid oxygen is magnetic.
This is liquid oxygen held between
the poles of a magnet.

When all the gases in the air have changed into liquid, the mixture is warmed up again. As the mixture reaches the temperatures shown in the table, each substance starts to boil on its own and comes off as a gas that can be collected separately. The name for this process is **fractional distillation**. Over 95% of the oxygen used in industry and medicine comes from liquefied air.

Melting points

Fractional distillation works with air because each substance has its own boiling point. Pure elements and pure compounds have exact boiling points and melting points. The drawings and the table give some examples.

We can use the melting point or boiling point to tell whether a substance is pure or is a mixture.

Mixtures do not have fixed boiling or melting points. You can tell that candle wax is a mixture by melting it and measuring the temperature when it melts. You find that it melts over a <u>range</u> of temperatures. It does not have an exact melting point. It is a mixture of substances.

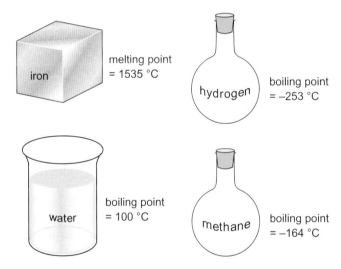

iron
melting point = 1535 °C

hydrogen
boiling point = −253 °C

water
boiling point = 100 °C

methane
boiling point = −164 °C

Substance	Boiling point	Melting point
sodium chloride	1413 °C	801 °C
oxygen	−183 °C	−214 °C
hydrogen chloride	−85 °C	−114 °C
mercury	357 °C	−39 °C

Question 4 5 6

You should already know | Outcomes | Keywords

In the beginning

You have seen what the atmosphere contains today. Some scientists think that the atmosphere was very different when it was formed about 4000 million years ago. They think that, when it formed, it was made from:

- mainly carbon dioxide gas;
- very little oxygen;
- small amounts of the gases methane and ammonia;
- some water vapour.

This is similar to the atmosphere on the planet Venus. Over 90% of the atmosphere on Venus consists of carbon dioxide. Humans and other animals could not live on Venus because of the lack of oxygen.

Question 1 2

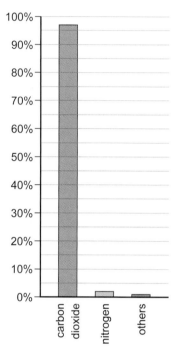

The atmosphere on Venus

We need oxygen, but carbon dioxide poisons us. So we wouldn't be able to live on Venus.

Changing the atmosphere

About 3500 million years ago, there were very tiny plant-like organisms living in the sea. These tiny living things used carbon dioxide to make their food and gave off oxygen as a waste product. The levels of oxygen in the atmosphere started to increase.

Gradually, larger living things evolved and eventually there were plants growing in the oceans and on the land. The plants used carbon dioxide to make their food in the process we call **photosynthesis**.

carbon dioxide + water ⟶ food + oxygen

The effect of this was to increase the amount of oxygen in the atmosphere and to reduce the amount of carbon dioxide.

Question 3 4

By 2200 million years ago, oxygen levels were high enough to make iron rust. Banded red ironstone rocks are evidence of this.

Locking up the carbon

Plants take in carbon dioxide and use the carbon in it to build material as they grow. Plants are at the beginning of the food chain so, when animals eat plants, the carbon passes from the plants into the animals. The carbon the plants take out of the atmosphere is locked up in the living things on the Earth.

When some living things die, they can turn into fossil fuels like coal or oil. Other dead material like wood can also be used as fuel. When fuel is burned, carbon dioxide is released back into the atmosphere.

When living things die and rot, carbon is also released into the atmosphere as methane gas. Methane gas is a compound. Its particles contain one carbon atom and four hydrogen atoms. Its formula is CH_4.

Sedimentary rocks like limestone also contain a lot of carbon that originally came from the bodies of sea creatures that formed the sedimentary rock.

This limestone is made from the remains of crinoids, or sea lilies. These animals are related to starfish.

Question 5

Human activity is changing the atmosphere

The level of carbon dioxide in the atmosphere has stayed about the same for a long time. There has been a balance between humans and animals producing carbon dioxide, and plants removing it.

Unfortunately, over the past 200 years, humans have been using fossil fuels. This has released carbon dioxide into the atmosphere and the levels are rising. Other human activities that result from our industrial society (such as changing limestone into lime) also release carbon dioxide into the atmosphere.

We began to use more and more fossil fuels during the industrial revolution. This began in the 1800s. The new machinery used coal, oil and gas.

Question 6

So what is the problem?

The levels of carbon dioxide are only increasing by small amounts but they are enough to cause the problem of **global warming**. As well as carbon dioxide, other gases we produce like methane also cause global warming. We refer to these gases as **greenhouse gases**. This is because the gases produce a blanket around the Earth that keeps in the heat from the Sun, a bit like the glass in a greenhouse.

Humans need to live without causing global warming. We also need to do this without using up resources that cannot be replaced. This is called **sustainable development**. Some scientists think that, unless we work very hard at this, the atmosphere will change enough to cause big problems. We may not be able to grow enough food, and sea levels may rise and swamp cities.

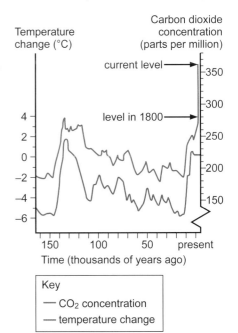

There is a link between the temperature of the Earth and the concentration of carbon dioxide in the atmosphere.

Question 7

You should already know   Outcomes   Keywords

Human development

While humans have been on the Earth they have:

- improved their understanding of how things work;
- discovered what substances things are made from;
- discovered how to make new substances from the raw materials on the Earth.

They have also developed technology to make life easier.

Improvements in medicine and food production means there are many more humans on the planet than there were.

As we develop our standard of living, we use more of the raw materials available on the Earth. We use many different raw materials.

- We use ores to make metals.
- We use oil to make plastics.
- We use oil coal and gas for energy.

We also produce a lot of waste. We pollute the environment with the materials that we throw away.

Human development causes problems.

- Many of the raw materials we use to make new compounds will eventually run out.
- Human development produces compounds like sulfur dioxide that damage the environment.
- Burning fossil fuels produces compounds, including carbon dioxide, which cause global warming.

In the past 200 years, the number of people on the planet has increased by about nine times.

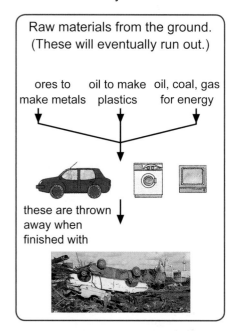

Raw materials from the ground. (These will eventually run out.)

ores to make metals   oil to make plastics   oil, coal, gas for energy

these are thrown away when finished with

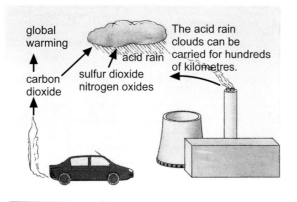

global warming

carbon dioxide

sulfur dioxide nitrogen oxides

acid rain

The acid rain clouds can be carried for hundreds of kilometres.

Scandinavia

Sulfur dioxide from Britain can produce acid rain in Scandinavia.

Carbon dioxide from Britain can affect the air all over the Earth.

Question 1   2

Needs and wants

Part of the problem is the difference between what people <u>need</u> and what people <u>want</u>.

Human beings have certain basic needs:

- food and water
- shelter
- clothing
- medicine
- energy sources for cooking and keeping warm.

In some parts of the world, particularly North America and Europe, we not only have the levels we need of these things but we have much more besides. Many people are very greedy and can only see the pleasure they get from a car that uses a lot of fuel, unnecessary air travel, luxury goods and a standard of living much higher than they actually need. There is a big difference between 'needing a new pair of trainers' and 'needing some food'.

Question 3

What is sustainable development?

There are more and more people on the Earth. We need to develop the way we produce food and provide water, shelter and energy to meet the growing demand. We need to manage this development in a way that does not damage the environment. If we damage the environment then we will not be able to keep the development going. Developing without damaging the environment or using up resources that cannot be replaced is called **sustainable development**.

The types of thing that governments are doing to support sustainable development include:

- making people more aware of recycling materials;
- setting out policies on the environment;
- drawing up international agreements to limit the levels of carbon dioxide produced;
- publicity to make people more aware of how their lifestyle affects the environment;
- increasing tax on certain types of cars and on fuel

The United Nations Environment Programme attempts to set standards and bring about co-operation between countries on environmental issues such as biodiversity, conservation of resources and climate change.

The UK government has policies on environmental issues such as biodiversity.

In the UK, local authorities have to have policies on issues such as land use and recycling.

As individuals, we can think about our own use of resources.

Review your work

Question 4 | 5

Summary ➡

You should already know

Outcomes

Keywords

Metals

Metals are very important materials. Very few metals occur in nature as pure metals. Most of the metals in the Earth are joined with other elements in compounds. These compounds that contain metals are often called <u>ores</u>. One very important application of science is getting metals out of their ores.

Haematite contains iron. This ore is a type of iron oxide (iron combined with oxygen).

It looks simple in the laboratory

Extracting a small sample of metal from an ore can seem easy in a laboratory. The diagram shows a common method of extracting a metal from an ore that contains a metal oxide. The idea is to heat the powdered ore with carbon powder. With some metals, the carbon and the ore will react and make carbon dioxide gas. This leaves the metal behind.

The word equation for the reaction is:

metal ore + carbon ⟶ carbon dioxide + metal

Malachite is copper carbonate (copper combined with carbon and oxygen).

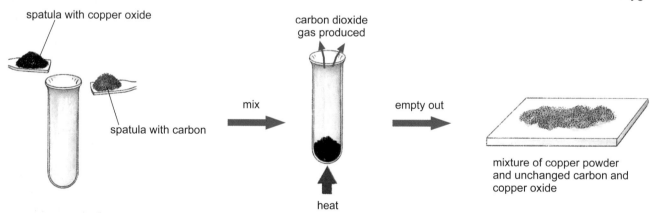

spatula with copper oxide

spatula with carbon

mix

carbon dioxide gas produced

empty out

heat

mixture of copper powder and unchanged carbon and copper oxide

The problems start when you try to do this on a large scale. Extracting the metal we need for today's society leads to **ethical** and **moral** problems. For example, ores are not just one pure compound – they contain a lot of other waste material. If you want a lot of metal then you need a lot of ore. The huge volumes of ore also have to be transported to the extraction plant. All these facts have consequences for the environment.

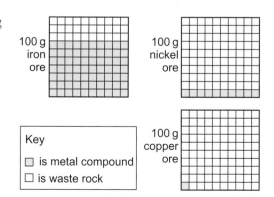

100 g iron ore

100 g nickel ore

100 g copper ore

Key

☐ is metal compound
☐ is waste rock

Question 1 2

The blast furnace

The blast furnace used to extract iron from iron ore has several problems:

- a lot of energy is required to run it;
- it produces atmospheric pollution;
- it produces visual pollution;
- it requires good road or rail links to supply raw materials;
- it produces a lot of waste.

Supplying iron ore means that it has to be dug out of the earth in the places where it occurs. The same idea applies to other ores. Mining these raw materials causes problems that have ethical and moral implications.

We pour carbon and iron oxide into the blast furnace. The iron oxide turns into iron metal. The reaction also makes carbon dioxide gas.

Iron ore mine in Australia. Mining metals and metal ores can make huge holes in the ground.

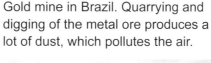

Gold mine in Brazil. Quarrying and digging of the metal ore produces a lot of dust, which pollutes the air.

Potash mine in Germany. Huge heaps of waste rock may be left behind. Wastes still contain metal compounds. These can pollute streams and harm living things.

Question 3 4

Recycling metals

One way we can help to solve some of the problems associated with the production of metals is by recycling the metals we use. Aluminium is a metal we use a lot. It is extracted from its ore using electricity.

If we recycle metals then we save energy. Saving energy means that we produce less pollution from power stations and have less impact on **global warming**.

Did you know that recycling just one aluminium drinks can save enough energy to run a TV for 2 hours?

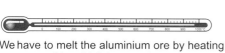

We have to melt the aluminium ore by heating it to a high temperature.

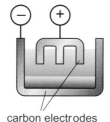

carbon electrodes

We extract aluminium from the molten ore using electricity.

Of course, recycling aluminium also uses energy, but only about a twentieth.

Question 5

8F.1

1 What do graphite and diamond have in common? What differences can you can discover between them?
Draw up a table comparing them.

2 **a** What do chalk and limestone have in common?
Find out how they differ.

   b List some key differences between limestone and alcohol.

3 What do we mean by the <u>formula</u> of a compound?
Give <u>one</u> example.

4 How many atoms are there in one molecule of calcium carbonate?
How can you work out the answer from its formula?

5 **a** What is the difference between a word equation and an equation using formulae?

   b What do you think the advantages of each type of equation are?
Give reasons for your answer.

6 What is the formula for water?
Explain how we know that this is the formula for water.

8F.2

1 Give <u>two</u> examples of reactions, with descriptions of ways in which the products differ from the reactants.

2 List the <u>five</u> clues that point to a chemical reaction taking place.

3 Give <u>four</u> different types of reaction.

4 Describe <u>one</u> way of showing that calcium oxide is a different substance from calcium carbonate.

5 **a** Give the chemical equation for what happens to calcium carbonate when you heat it strongly.

   b What is the name for this type of reaction?

   c Explain why you might easily think that no reaction has taken place when you heat calcium carbonate strongly.

6 Find out why quicklime is a useful substance.

8F.3

1   What is meant by the term <u>mixture</u>?
Give <u>three</u> examples.

2   Air is often described as a mixture of gases.
Explain what this means and list <u>three</u> of the gases you already
know are in the mixture called air.

3   a   Why could it be misleading to describe mineral water as 'pure'?

    b   What is the difference between the way a supermarket label uses
the word <u>pure</u> and the way it is used in science?

4   How do we know that seawater is a mixture?

5   a   What happens to a mixture of water and dissolved salts when the
water evaporates?

    b   Why do you think this happens?

    c   Find out how people collect sea salt for cooking with.

8F.4

1   a   Which <u>two</u> gases make up most of the air?

    b   State the approximate percentages of these two gases in air.

    c   About what percentage of the air is occupied by everything else?

2   a   What can cause food to spoil?

    b   Why do you think that nitrogen is useful in preventing
food spoilage?

3   What properties of carbon dioxide make it useful in fighting fire?

4   If you cooled a sample of air down to −100 °C, what state would
each different part of the mixture be in?
Give reasons for your answers.

5   a   What is meant by the term <u>fractional distillation</u>?

    b   How is it used to get oxygen from the air?

    c   Find out <u>one</u> other important use of fractional distillation.

6   Describe <u>one</u> way of telling if a substance is pure or a mixture.

8F.5

1 Describe the main difference between the atmosphere 4000 million years ago and the atmosphere today.

2 Why could humans not have lived on the Earth 4000 million years ago?

3 What caused oxygen levels in the atmosphere to increase?

4 Write down the word equation for photosynthesis.

5 Where does all the carbon in our bodies come from originally?

6 What human activity has caused a rise in the level of carbon dioxide gas in the atmosphere in the past 200 years?

7 What is the problem with increasing the level of carbon dioxide gas in the atmosphere?

8F.6

1 What developments have led to there being more people on the planet in 2000 than there were in 1800?

2 Give three problems that are caused by human development.

3 List the basic needs for human beings.

4 What is meant by sustainable development?

5 What types of thing are governments doing to encourage sustainable development?

8F.HSW

1   A metal ore contains a lot of waste material, and this causes a problem at the extraction plant.
    Why is this?

2   A lot of material has to be transported to and from an extraction plant.

    a   What problems will this cause for people living nearby?

    b   Suggest why some people will think that having the plant nearby has advantages.

    (Hint: include ideas about health problems, noise pollution, effects on house structures and the value of property.)

3   List some of the problems for people living near a blast furnace.
    (Hint: a blast furnace may produce a lot of noise and light. The raw materials need to be brought in, and the products and waste need to be removed. It will probably operate 24 hours a day.)

4   a   Write a draft of a letter that you might send to your MP objecting to a blast furnace being built near to where you live.

    b   What sort of points might be made by people in favour of building the blast furnace?

5   Why is it a good idea to recycle aluminium cans?

You should already know | Outcomes | Keywords

Different rocks, different properties

Scientists who study rocks are called **geologists**. Geologists study a wide range of materials that they call 'rock'. Some rocks are very hard. Some are soft and crumbly.

Rocks occur in all sorts of shapes and sizes. They come in a wide range of colours.

Limestone is a fairly hard rock made from calcium carbonate.

Marble is a rock made from calcium carbonate crystals. You can smooth and polish it.

Even though these rocks look different, they all contain the compound calcium carbonate.

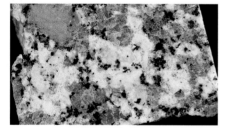

Granite is a very hard rock.

Sandstone is a soft rock. You can scratch it with your nails.

Slate is a hard rock made of layers. It splits easily into sheets.

Most rocks are made of a mixture of grains of different sizes.

We call things like 'soft', 'crumbly', 'grain size', 'colour' and all the other things used to tell the difference between rocks <u>properties</u>.

There are many different types of rock. They all have different properties.

Some of the types of rock are made from calcium carbonate. Even though they are made from the same compound, they have different properties. This is because of the different ways in which the particles of calcium carbonate are arranged and because of other substances that help to make up the rocks.

Because the rocks have different properties, they have different names.

Question 1 / 2 / 3

Rocks like sponges

Rocks are not soft like sponge, but some rocks do have very tiny gaps between the grains that make them up. These gaps will let liquid and gas pass through the rock, a bit like water through a sponge.

Rocks that let liquid and gas pass through them are called **porous** rocks. Sandstone is an example of a porous rock.

Some rocks have grains that fit very closely together with no spaces between them. These rocks do not let water soak into them. We say that they are <u>non-porous</u>.

Chalk is a porous rock.

Question 4

One important thing that happens because there are porous and non-porous rocks is that oil gets trapped in the Earth's surface. As a result, geologists can work out where oil might be found and people can drill down to collect this valuable resource.

Oil forms underground in tiny drops spread through lots of porous rocks. Because the rocks are porous, the water and oil can move through the rocks. The oil floats on top of the water.

Where the rocks are curved into a dome shape and a layer of non-porous rock lies on top of porous rock, you can get oil trapped in the top of the porous rock.

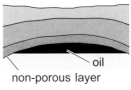

Oil drops move up though the water in porous rocks.

Rocks and minerals

The grains that make up a rock can be made from different substances. These different substances are called **minerals**. If you look closely at some rocks, you can see the different minerals.

In some rocks, the minerals form small crystals. In other rocks, the minerals form much larger crystals.

Granite is a rock made from three different minerals that are in quite large crystals. Granite is sometimes polished and used as a decorative stone because of the appearance of its minerals.

The three minerals in granite are called quartz, feldspar and mica.

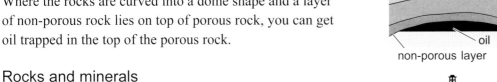

When the oil reaches a non-porous rock layer, it can't rise any further. The oil is trapped under the dome of non-porous rock.

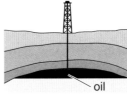

You drill through the non-porous rock to get the oil.

Question 5 **6**

Mineral	Properties
quartz	very hard, looks glassy, often a milky white colour, cannot be scratched with a knife
feldspar	there are lots of different feldspars, often seen in pink or white crystals
mica	small black crystals

You should already know

Outcomes

Keywords

Rocks change

Rocks do not stay the same for ever. Over a period of time, they very slowly get worn away by lots of different things. Rain, frost and temperature changes can all change the shapes of rocks.

When rocks are worn away by these things, we call it **weathering**.

The statue in the photograph is made from carved limestone. The rain has eaten away the rock over many years.

Question 1 2

How does rain attack limestone?

- Rainwater is a very weak acid.
- Limestone is made from calcium carbonate.
- Calcium carbonate reacts with acid to produce carbon dioxide gas, water and a salt.
- When acid rain reacts with limestone, the carbon dioxide goes into the air and the other products are washed away by the rain.

In the case of rainwater eating away limestone, a chemical reaction happens. This is an example of something called **chemical weathering**.

Rain is a very weak acid so the reaction is only very slight. It takes many years until you notice the effect on a rock or building made from limestone. That means that, even though it suffers from chemical weathering, limestone is a very useful building material.

Carbon dioxide is given off.

Chemical weathering is a very slow process. You can see the effect if you look at the changes in a limestone wall or in the carvings on gravestones over many years.

Chemical weathering is happening faster than it used to because the way we live now produces more gases that make acid rain.

Weather changes limestone. Acid rain makes it change even faster.

Question 3 4

Physical weathering

Physical weathering does not involve a chemical reaction. This is where the rock is broken up by forces caused by changes in temperature. One way this works involves water freezing in cracks in the rock.

Water occupies a larger volume when it freezes. We say that it expands. This is why ice floats on water. This is unusual behaviour – most substances contract when they freeze. When water changes to ice, the **expansion** can produce very large forces.

You can show this by freezing water in a bottle. The bottle will be broken by the expanding ice. You can even do this with a bottle made of cast iron and that will break too!

Rainwater gets into any cracks that are in the surface of a rock. If the temperature drops low enough, the rainwater will freeze, which makes the crack a little larger. This means that more water will be able to get in when the temperature rises.

The process repeats until eventually a bit of the rock breaks off. Sometimes, quite large boulders break off, as the picture shows.

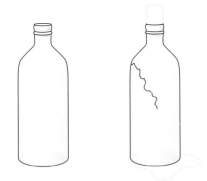

The water in this bottle changed to ice.

water

The force of expansion can break off large boulders.

Heat alone

Heat from the Sun can make the surface of a rock get a little bit bigger. We call this expansion.

When the temperature falls at night, the rock gets smaller again. We say that it contracts.

Repeated expanding and contracting doesn't just crack the surface of a rock. It can cause the whole rock to crack.

Other ways of changing rocks

Wind and running water can also wear away rocks.

Wind blows fine particles of dust and sand against rocks. This wears away their surface.

Plants can root themselves in the cracks in rocks. The plant holds moisture. The shade from the plant also means parts of the rock surface reach different temperatures when the Sun shines. Both of these things can increase physical weathering.

Some animals, like limpets, make an acid that attacks rocks.

Weathering that is caused by plants or animals is called **biotic weathering**.

This rock has been cracked by hot days and cold nights in the desert.

A scree slope is a lot of small rock pieces produced by weathering.

The holes in this rock have been worn away by sand blown by the wind.

Question 5 **6**

You should already know

Outcomes

Keywords

Moving pieces of rock around

Weathering can cause rocks to break up into small bits. These are called **rock fragments**. You need a force to make a rock fragment move from one place to another. There are usually three things that can provide the force if the right size of rock fragment is in the right place at the right time:

- gravity;
- wind;
- water.

Gravity makes loose rock fragments fall or roll down slopes.

Wind can blow tiny rock fragments from one place to another.

Water in the form of rain washes small rock fragments down slopes.

Once rock fragments are washed into a stream or river, small fragments get carried away by the flow of water and larger ones get left behind.

Question 1 2

Forming sediments

The speed of a flowing stream or river depends on things like the slope of the land. If a stream or river is flowing quickly then it can move quite large rocks. Streams or rivers that flow more slowly can only move tiny rock fragments like fine sand.

When the speed of a stream or river drops because the slope changes, some of the rock fragments will settle on the stream or river bed. We call this process **deposition**. The rock fragments that settle on the bottom are called **deposits**. The deposits build up to form **sediments**.

The pictures show the sediments deposited at different stages of a river's journey.

Question 3 4

In the hills, streams flow quickly. Streams carry smaller rock fragments away and leave the large fragments behind.

Further downstream, we see beaches made of pebbles.

On flatter land, the river flows more slowly, so it deposits sand.

The river deposits fine sand and mud as it gets nearer to the sea.

Changes in rock fragments

Rock fragments are made by weathering. When they are made, the rock fragments have sharp edges and corners. We say that they are <u>angular</u>.

As the angular rock fragments are moved along by gravity, wind or water, they knock against each other, a bit like the particles in a gas. This causes the sharp corners and edges to become more rounded.

This process of rocks knocking and rubbing against each other produces wearing, which is called **abrasion**.

We sometimes use the same idea to clean stone walls and pavements by blowing jets of air mixed with sand at them at high speed. This is called <u>sand blasting</u>.

These pebbles have been worn smooth by rubbing against each other in water.

Question 5 \ 6

Layers of sediment

If you stir up a beaker of water that contains a mixture of different sized rock fragments, you get an interesting result. The larger, heavier fragments settle to the bottom first and the smaller, lighter fragments settle on top.

Because the particles settle out in turn, you get different layers forming, with the larger, heavier fragments at the bottom.

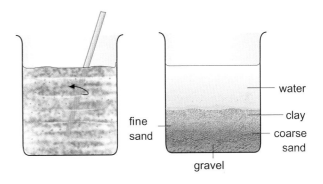

The same effect happens in nature. Rivers deposit sediments on the sea bed. The order of the layers depends on more than fragment size because rivers carry different sediments at different times. A slow-moving river will carry sand. The same river in flood will carry a lot of stones and mud. Over the millions of years that sediments are deposited, there are many changes in what the rivers carry. The important idea is that the sediments at the bottom were deposited before the sediments that are on top.

You can see this in the picture. First a layer of mud was deposited, then a layer of sand and then another layer of mud.

As the layers build up over millions of years, the older layers get squashed and harden. These form rocks we call **sedimentary rocks**, like mudstone, sandstone and clay.

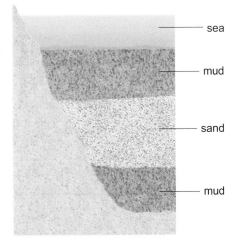

Sometimes rivers carry sand into the sea. At other times they carry mud.

Question 7 \ 8

Check your progress

Rocks from dissolved solids

Rock fragments are produced by physical weathering. The rock fragments carried by rivers form layers of deposit on the sea bed. Over millions of years, these layers get compressed and form new sedimentary rocks.

Chemical weathering does not produce rock fragments. It produces salts that dissolve in rainwater and get washed into streams and rivers. If you look on the label of a bottle of mineral water, it gives a list of the dissolved salts. Some of these are the products of chemical weathering.

Mineral water, showing the dissolved salts.

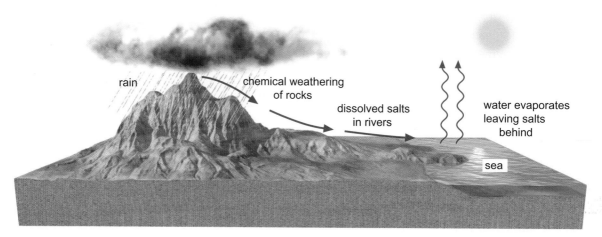

How dissolved solids become concentrated in seas and lakes.

When water evaporates from the sea or from a lake, the salts that were dissolved in it get left behind as crystals. The crystals form parts of the sediment in the sea and therefore part of sedimentary rocks.

In some parts of the world, the evaporation from lakes can be so fast that crystals form at their edges.

Question 1 2

Stories in rocks

When animals with hard parts like shells or skeletons die, the soft parts of their bodies decay away. The hard parts that are left behind can end up in sedimentary rocks. We call these remains **fossils**.

Fossils are very common in sedimentary rocks like coal or limestone.

Water evaporates from this soda lake faster than it flows in. As water evaporates, crystals of salts are deposited.

Fossils can help us to work out something about how a rock formed. In the case of limestone, the fossils are from tiny sea creatures. Limestone must be a rock that was formed under the sea.

This piece of coal has the fossilised remains of a plant in it.

Fossils in limestone.

Coal contains fossils of plants similar to ferns. This means that coal did not form under the sea. We think coal formed when trees and plants were buried in the mud of swamps, millions of years ago.

We can use fossils to date rocks. If rocks from different areas have the same fossils in them then scientists believe that the rocks must be about the same age.

Sometimes, you can tell from their shape that rocks formed where there was running water, like in a river bed. Some sandstone has ripple marks in it which resemble the sand ripples on a beach.

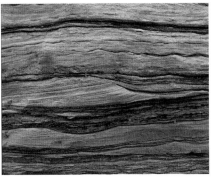

This rock formed in a river delta. The stripes in the rock are called <u>current banding</u>.

The rocks in a cliff face take millions of years to form. The drawing shows the rocks in a cliff face. It tells us a lot.

- Shale is the oldest layer, because it is at the bottom.
- The limestone contains coral fossils so, at the time that it was made, the sea must have been clear, warm and shallow because those are the conditions that coral needs to grow.
- We can tell the sediments formed in a clear sea for a long period of time because we have a thick layer of light sandstone.
- On top of the sandstone, there is a layer of salt, which means that the sea in that region must have dried out for some period of time.

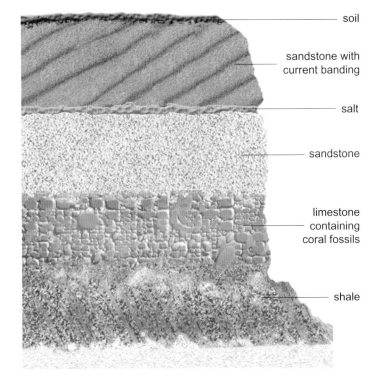

soil

sandstone with current banding

salt

sandstone

limestone containing coral fossils

shale

It is important to remember that the formation of rocks and fossils takes place over millions of years. This sort of timescale is very hard to imagine. Rather than use centuries and years, scientists sometimes use a scale called **geological time**, which breaks the past 600 million years or so up into sections.

Question 3 4 5

Review your work

Summary ➡

You should already know

Outcomes

Keywords

Range

The **range** of measurements you make in an investigation is the difference between the smallest measurement and the largest.

narrow range

broad range

It is important to make measurement over a large enough range.
If your range is too small then you might miss an important result.

Two students do an experiment on a piece of limestone to see how the concentration of acid affects how long it takes to dissolve.

$100cm^3$ acid and $0cm^3$ water	$80cm^3$ acid and $20cm^3$ water
$90cm^3$ acid and $10cm^3$ water	$81cm^3$ acid and $19cm^3$ water
$80cm^3$ acid and $20cm^3$ water	$82cm^3$ acid and $18cm^3$ water
$70cm^3$ acid and $30cm^3$ water	$83cm^3$ acid and $17cm^3$ water
$60cm^3$ acid and $40cm^3$ water	$84cm^3$ acid and $16cm^3$ water
$50cm^3$ acid and $50cm^3$ water	$85cm^3$ acid and $15cm^3$ water
$40cm^3$ acid and $60cm^3$ water	$86cm^3$ acid and $14cm^3$ water
$30cm^3$ acid and $70cm^3$ water	$87cm^3$ acid and $13cm^3$ water
$20cm^3$ acid and $80cm^3$ water	$88cm^3$ acid and $12cm^3$ water
$10cm^3$ acid and $90cm^3$ water	$89cm^3$ acid and $11cm^3$ water
$0cm^3$ acid and $100cm^3$ water	$90cm^3$ acid and $10cm^3$ water

These are the acid concentrations that Lauren suggested.

These are the acid concentrations that Daniel suggested.

Crushed limestone dissolves faster in strong acid.

Question 1 2

Consistency

Once you have carried out an experiment, you need to be sure that your **conclusion** fits in with the **evidence** from your results. We say that the conclusion and the evidence need to be **consistent**.

The experiment shown below is investigating the effect of freezing and thawing on three different rocks. The aim is to understand what happens during freeze–thaw weathering.

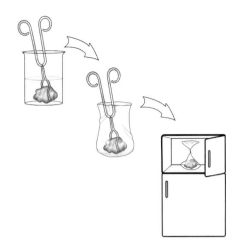

The rock is dipped in water and put in a bag in the freezer for 24 hours. The process is then repeated.

The results of the experiment are shown in the table.

Rock	Observations		
	At start	After three freezes	After eight freezes
limestone	two small cracks	cracks have grown slightly longer	one piece has broken off, and a few more cracks have appeared
granite	no cracks	no cracks	no cracks
slate	many cracks between layers	one layer has broken off	the rock is now in five pieces

Three pupils doing the experiment think about three different possible conclusions.

- Freeze–thaw weathering affects limestone the most.
- Freeze–thaw weathering affects granite the most.
- Freeze–thaw weathering affects slate the most.

The conclusion that is consistent with the evidence is the third one – that freeze–thaw weathering affects slate the most.

Are your conclusions consistent with the evidence, Holmes?

 Question 3   4

8G.1

1 What is a geologist?

2 Give <u>three</u> examples of the different properties of rocks.

3 **a** Explain how rocks can appear different even if they are made from the same compound.

   b Give <u>one</u> example of two rocks that this applies to.

4 **a** What is the difference between a porous rock and a non-porous rock?

   b Explain why the difference occurs.

5 Describe how porous and non-porous rocks play a part in finding oil underground.

6 **a** What is a mineral?

   b Give <u>three</u> examples of minerals and describe where they can be seen.

8G.2

1 What is <u>weathering</u>?

2 What has caused the weathering of the statue in the photograph?

3 **a** What is <u>chemical weathering</u>?

   b Give <u>one</u> example of how it can happen.

4 Cleopatra's Needle is a stone carving that was brought to London from Egypt just over 100 years ago. It had stood in the desert for thousands of years. When it arrived in London, the carvings on it were very clear. They are now very weathered.
   Explain why that has happened so quickly.

5 Describe the process of physical weathering caused by rainwater freezing in cracks.

6 **a** What is meant by <u>biotic weathering</u>?

   b Give <u>one</u> example of how it can happen.

8G.3

1 Describe how rock fragments are formed.

2 Describe <u>three</u> ways that rock fragments are moved in nature.

3 What is meant by the term <u>deposition</u>?

4 Describe how sediments form on the beds of rivers, and explain why some sizes of rock fragment travel further than others.

continued

5 What is meant by the term <u>abrasion</u>?

6 Give <u>two</u> examples of the use of abrasion.

7 Explain why the sediments carried by rivers change from time to time.

8 **a** How do sedimentary rocks form?

   b Give <u>three</u> examples of sedimentary rocks.

8G.4

1 Where are many rock fragments eventually deposited to form sedimentary rock?

2 What is produced by chemical weathering and how does this material transfer to sedimentary rock?

3 **a** What is a fossil?

   b Where are fossils found?

   c Give <u>two</u> examples of where fossils are found.

4 How do geologists know that limestone is a sedimentary rock formed under the seabed?

5 **a** Why do you think scientists use a geological timescale to describe the changes in rocks rather than centuries?

   b Find out what the main periods of geological time are.

8G.HSW

1 **a** What is meant by the word <u>range</u> when a set of observations are made?

   b Why is it important to use a range that is large enough?

2 **a** What is the difference between the range of concentrations suggested by Lauren and the range suggested by Daniel?

   b Why might Lauren's suggestion show more clearly that the time limestone takes to dissolve is affected by the concentration of the acid?

3 What do these words mean?

   a evidence

   b conclusion

   c consistent

4 **a** Explain why the third conclusion is the one that is consistent with the evidence.

   b Write another conclusion that is consistent with the evidence.

8H.1 Changing rocks (HSW)

You have learned how looking at rocks can tell us things about the past.

- The weather breaks down rocks.
- Rivers carry rock fragments to the sea and into lakes.
- Layers of sediment build up on the floors of seas and lakes.
- The layers of sediment bury older layers and squash them.

These things are happening all the time. They have been happening on the Earth for over 4000 million years.

When rocks are made from old sediments being squashed by new sediments, we call them sedimentary rocks.

This sedimentary rock is made from many thin layers of sediment. The lines can be seen in the rock.

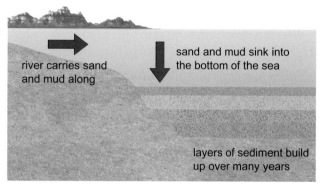

Layers of sediment form on the sea bed.

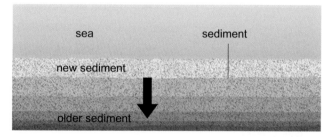

The weight of new sediments presses down on the older sediments. This pressure squeezes the water out and compresses the sediments. Chemical changes cement the fragments together, forming solid rock.

The clues that tell us a rock is sedimentary are:

- the rock has layers;
- the rock contains fossils;
- the rock is made of grains or particles that are cemented together;
- the rock is porous.

Some sedimentary rocks show only some of these clues and not all of them.

Question 1   2

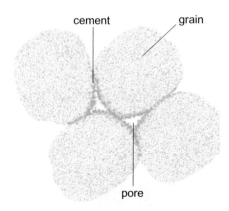

The grains of sedimentary rocks do not interlock. There are often pores or spaces between the grains. We say that sedimentary rocks are <u>porous</u>.

Changing sedimentary rocks

When sedimentary rocks get buried deeper and deeper in the Earth over millions of years, they are subjected to massive levels of **pressure** and very **high temperatures**.

This can make them change their structure and form new types of rock. These new types of rock are called **metamorphic** rocks.

The name metamorphic is made up from two parts:

- meta means 'changes';
- morph means 'form'.

Metamorphic means 'changed form'.

Metamorphic rocks are usually harder than sedimentary rocks.

Question 3   4

Slate is a metamorphic rock that forms from shale.

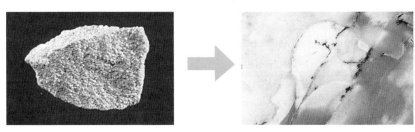

You can see rounded grains and pores in limestone. Marble is harder, with a granular, sugary texture and no pore spaces.

Sandstone is made up of grains of sand. Quartzite is harder, with a sugary texture.

The heat that changes rocks comes from the molten rock called **magma** that is deep under the Earth's crust. Sometimes, this magma forces its way up into the Earth's crust. The rocks that are near it get very hot and this can make rocks change into metamorphic rocks.

The Earth's crust is always moving, very slowly. Over millions of years, the layers of rock in the Earth's surface get twisted and squashed. This produces a lot of pressure. You can sometimes see the effect on layers of rock on exposed cliff faces.

As you go deeper under the Earth's surface, the pressure and temperature increase. This South African gold mine is so hot that the miners can only work for a few hours at a time.

Molten rock heats up the rocks near to it.

How limestone is changed to marble.

Diagram labels: other rock; limestone layer; limestone changed into marble here; hot magma; other rock; other rock

Question 5   6

Movements of the Earth's crust cause heating and squashing of rocks.

When solids get hot enough, the particles they are made from have enough energy to change places. The solid melts and changes into a liquid.

This happens at 0 °C when ice changes to water. It happens at about 1000 °C for rocks like granite. Liquid rock is called **magma**. A large part of the middle of the Earth is made of this molten rock. The crust of the Earth, which is made of solid rock, is very thin compared with the size of the Earth. If the Earth was the size of an orange, the crust of solid rock would be like the orange peel.

When magma cools, it forms solid rock. Because magma is a mixture of different minerals, it often forms crystals of the different minerals when it solidifies. You can see the crystals in the rocks that form. Look at the photographs below.

When a rock is made by magma cooling into a solid it is called an **igneous** rock. The word <u>igneous</u> comes from the Latin word for fire, *ignis*.

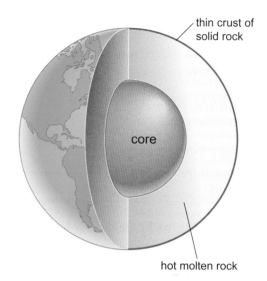

thin crust of solid rock

core

hot molten rock

Cross-section through the Earth.

Question 1

Crystal size

If you evaporate salt water, you get salt **crystals**. You get much larger crystals if you let the water evaporate slowly.

The same type of thing happens when magma cools. If magma cools slowly, it forms large crystals. If magma cools quickly, it forms small crystals.

these crystals formed quickly

these crystals formed slowly

The size of the crystals depends on how quickly you evaporate the water from the solution.

Granite.

Basalt.

Pumice is an igneous rock that has cooled so fast that you can see gas bubbles but no crystals.

Question 2

Some magmas cool more slowly than others

There are basically three situations in which magma cools and forms igneous rock.

- The magma cools deep underground. Because it is surrounded by hot rock, it cools very slowly. It will form large crystals.
- The magma forces its way nearer to the surface through cracks in rocks. This magma cools quickly. It forms medium sized or small crystals depending upon how fast it cools.
- The magma comes out of a hole in the Earth's surface as a liquid and cools rapidly when it emerges. It will form very small crystals or even not form any crystals at all.

Volcanoes

We call magma that reaches the Earth's surface **lava**. When lava emerges on the Earth's surface, we say that it **erupts**.

Some lavas are very runny and spread over a large area. Other lavas are less runny and build up when they come out of the Earth, forming a cone of rock that we call a **volcano**.

Sometimes the magma solidifies inside a volcano. It acts like a giant plug. Gases are trapped under the plug. The pressure can build up until the plug cannot hold back the material underneath.

When this happens, there is a violent eruption and gases, solids and molten lava burst out of the top of the volcano like froth from a shaken fizzy drink.

This type of eruption produces a lot of volcanic ash, which can form a large ash cone.

This type of eruption happened at Vesuvius in Italy in AD 79. It buried the nearby town of Pompeii in volcanic ash. You can visit the ruins today and see how life in the town suddenly came to a stop when the ash hit it.

 Question 3   **4**

The volcano in the diagram has formed by layers of lava emerging and solidifying, followed by eruptions of ash, all forming a cone of new rock.

Volcanoes can also erupt under the sea. Sometimes, when they do, they produce a new island. The island of Surtsey is off the south coast of Iceland. It erupted and formed in 1963. The first signs were clouds of steam emerging from the sea. It is now a nature reserve.

 Question 5

Lava from a volcano in Hawaii.

Mount St Helens is an ash cone. Ash was blown out in a cloud.

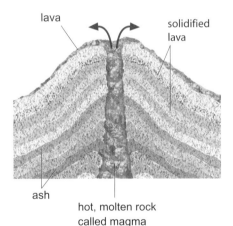
lava   solidified lava

ash

hot, molten rock called magma

Some volcanic cones form from ash and lava.

Surtsey erupted under the sea and formed a new island.

Check your progress

You should already know
)
Outcomes
)
Keywords
)

Three main types of rock

There are three main types of rock.

- **Sedimentary**:
  Formed when sediments are compressed and cemented together by pressure under the sea bed.
- **Metamorphic**:
  Formed when rocks are subjected to high levels of heat and pressure deep inside the Earth's crust.
- **Igneous**:
  Formed when liquid magma cools and solidifies into rock.

All three types of rock will form rock fragments if they are exposed to the weather. Rock fragments are moved by gravity, wind and water until some of them end up as sediments in the sea. They then make new sedimentary rock.

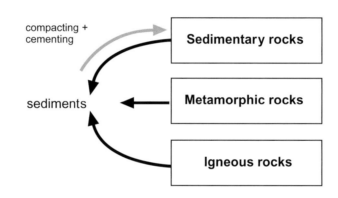

As new rocks are made, the older rocks sink deeper in the Earth's crust. Some are changed into metamorphic rock by heat and pressure. Eventually, the deepest and oldest rocks melt into the magma underneath the Earth's crust.

This means that the material from those rocks can be recycled into new igneous rock when any of the magma emerges as lava on the Earth's surface.

This constant recycling of the material in rocks is called the **rock cycle**.

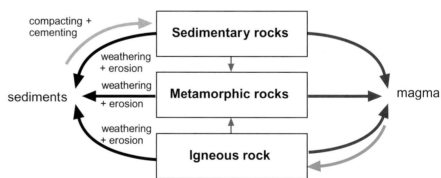

Question 1) 2)

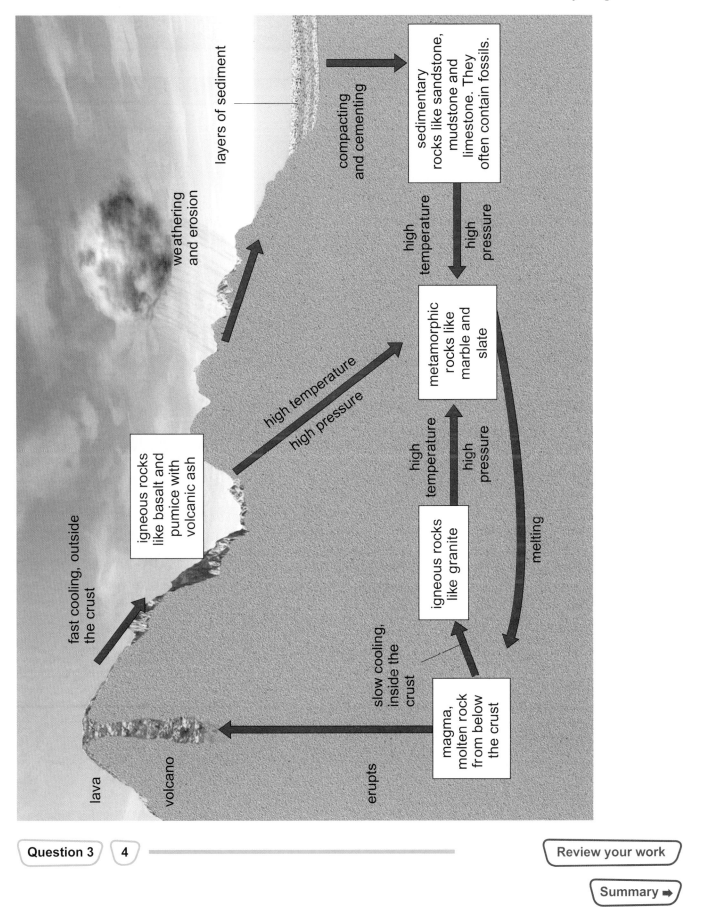

layers of sediment

compacting and cementing

sedimentary rocks like sandstone, mudstone and limestone. They often contain fossils.

high temperature

high pressure

weathering and erosion

igneous rocks like basalt and pumice with volcanic ash

high temperature

high pressure

metamorphic rocks like marble and slate

fast cooling, outside the crust

high temperature

high pressure

melting

igneous rocks like granite

slow cooling, inside the crust

magma, molten rock from below the crust

lava

volcano

erupts

Question 3   4

Review your work

Summary →

You should already know

Outcomes

Keywords

Changing ideas about the Earth

Our ideas about what the Earth is made from have gradually changed.

People used to believe the Earth was only a few thousand years old and never changed. When geologists worked out how rocks formed, they realised that the Earth was much older. The first theory was that it formed when hot molten rock cooled over millions of years. This theory explained mountains and valleys.

However, geologists worked out that the Earth had to be over 4000 million years old. If the Earth was that old, it would have cooled so much that the middle would be completely solid. We know from volcanoes that this is not true. We also know that the Earth produces heat in its centre because it contains radioactive materials. This evidence contradicted the shrinking Earth theory.

Vibrations from earthquakes and explosions travel through the Earth. Scientists detect these at different places around the Earth and think up theories to explain what they observe.

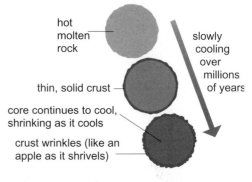

hot molten rock

slowly cooling over millions of years

thin, solid crust

core continues to cool, shrinking as it cools

crust wrinkles (like an apple as it shrivels)

The shrinking Earth theory.

A moving crust

In 1912, a German scientist called Alfred Wegener suggested that, millions of years ago, all the land on the Earth's surface was in one large continent. He suggested that this land had split and moved apart over millions of years to make the continents that we have today. This is sometimes called **continental drift**.

Wegener had some evidence to back up his ideas.

- The shape of the continents fitted together.
- When they were fitted together, the places where particular rocks are found on different continents line up.
- Similar fossils are found on different continents where they fit together.

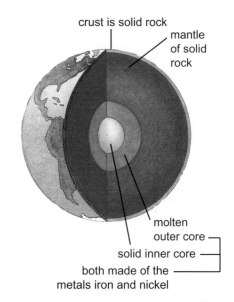

crust is solid rock

mantle of solid rock

molten outer core

solid inner core

both made of the metals iron and nickel

Scientists think this is what the Earth is like inside. This model explains all the observations.

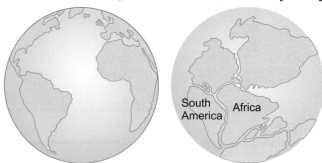

The Earth today

The Earth millions of years ago

South America   Africa

We think the continents we know today all broke away from a larger land mass millions of years ago.

Question 1 2

Another theory

Wegener's idea was not accepted by everyone, mainly because he could not explain why the continents had drifted apart. He was also a scientist whose area of study was actually the weather and not a geologist, so many Earth scientists were prejudiced against him and did not want to accept his ideas.

In the 1960s, a new theory was developed to explain observations of rocks on the ocean floor. The rocks have patterns of magnetism in them. To explain this, geologists thought up the theory of **tectonic plates**.

In this theory, the Earth's surface is made of several large plates that are slowly moving about on the molten magma underneath them. These plates can move up to a few centimetres in a year.

This theory explains Wegener's idea of continental drift. It also explains some other observations.

The places where the plates meet are called <u>plate boundaries</u>. According to the theory, this is where the plates are moving apart or pushing together. This can cause sudden movements, which produce earthquakes and volcanoes.

If you look at a map of the Earth and plot where earthquakes and volcanoes happen, the sites match the plate boundaries.

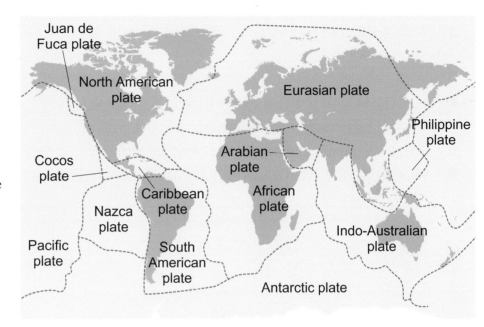

Tectonic plates.

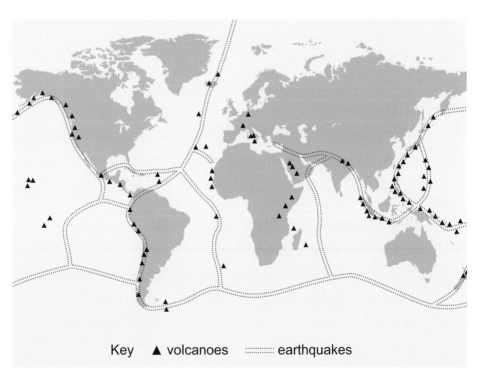

Key   ▲ volcanoes   ⋯⋯⋯ earthquakes

Where earthquakes and volcanoes happen around the world.

 Question 3   4

8H.1

1 Summarise how sedimentary rocks form under the sea bed.

2 What are <u>four</u> of the clues that show that a rock is a sedimentary rock?

3 What can make the structure of a sedimentary rock change?

4 **a** Explain what is meant by the term <u>metamorphic rock</u>.

   b Give <u>two</u> examples of metamorphic rocks.

5 Where does the heat come from to produce metamorphic rocks?

6 What evidence have we got that there can be very large pressures in the Earth's crust?

8H.2

1 **a** What is meant by an <u>igneous rock</u>?

   b Describe how an igneous rock is formed.

2 **a** What is the difference in crystal size between granite and basalt?

   b What does this tell us about how the two rocks formed?

3 What is the difference between lava and magma?

4 **a** What else is produced by a volcano apart from lava?

   b What effects can these substances have?

5 **a** Describe how a volcano can form a new island.

   b Suggest how the island could eventually develop life on it.

8H.3

1 **a** What are the <u>three</u> main types of rock?

   b How is each type formed?

2 What is the name for the constant recycling of the material in rocks?

3 Which rocks melt into the magma in the rock cycle?

4 Describe the journey of a mineral from a piece of granite on a cliff over millions and millions of years as it gradually travels through each type of rock.

8H.HSW

1   a   How did the shrinking Earth theory explain the appearance of mountains and valleys on the Earth's surface?

    b   What was the problem with the theory that led to it being eventually rejected?

2   What evidence did Wegener have to support his idea of continental drift?

3   What is the idea that is now used to explain continental drift and the location of earthquakes and volcanoes?

4   Find out what the San Andreas fault is and why people who live in San Francisco are concerned about any tectonic plate movements.

8I.1 Measuring how hot things are

You should already know   Outcomes   Keywords

Temperature

People judge how hot or cold things are by the feelings they get from their skin. There is a problem with this: your estimate depends on where your skin has just been! If you move from a hot place to a cool place, you will think that it is colder than it actually is.

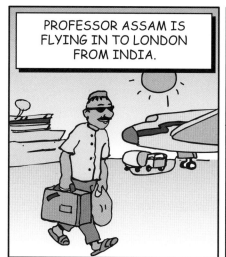

PROFESSOR ASSAM IS FLYING IN TO LONDON FROM INDIA.

HIS OLD FRIEND DOCTOR CHILBLAIN, AN EXPERT IN LOW TEMPERATURE PHYSICS, LEAVES HIS LAB IN ICELAND ABOUT THE SAME TIME.

THEY ARE BOTH MET AT HEATHROW BY HIS COUSIN INDIRA WHO LIVES IN LONDON.

PROFESSOR ASSAM FEELS COLD. DOCTOR CHILBLAIN FEELS TOO HOT. INDIRA THINKS THEY ARE BOTH WRONG. AFTER ALL IT IS JUNE AND VERY PLEASANT WEATHER IN LONDON.

We use the word **temperature** to describe how hot or cold something is. To get an accurate temperature measurement, you need something that always gives the same answer no matter where it has just been. Your skin is no good for this! We use an instrument called a **thermometer**.

Question 1 2

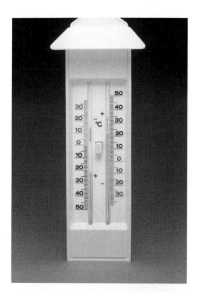

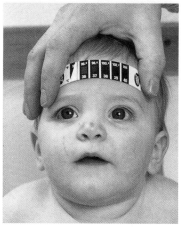

Two different types of thermometer.

Types of thermometer

There are many different types of thermometer. Some use a liquid that expands and contracts when the temperature changes. These are called liquid-in-glass thermometers.

Digital thermometers use electronic components and circuits to sense the temperature. These are easier to read and less fragile than liquid-in-glass thermometers. Their disadvantages include a higher cost and the need for a battery or power supply.

The first type of thermometer was invented by Galileo in 1592. It used the expansion and contraction of air to show the temperature. It was not very accurate, but it was better than nothing.

It took about another 150 years until a thermometer like the liquid-in-glass thermometer we use today was invented.

A liquid-in-glass and a digital thermometer.

 Question 3

Galileo's thermometer.

Temperature scales

Many different scales have been used to measure temperature. The most common scale we use today is called the **Celsius** scale.

Some countries still use a scale called the Fahrenheit scale. If you listen to weather forecasts or read a cookery book, the temperature is sometimes given in both Celsius and Fahrenheit.

Both these scales give the temperature in divisions called **degrees**. The degrees on the Fahrenheit scale are smaller than the degrees on the Celsius scale.

A much more important scale is sometimes used in science. It is called the Kelvin scale. This has the same size of degree as the Celsius scale.

Situation	Celsius temperature	Fahrenheit temperature	Kelvin temperature
lowest possible temperature	−273 °C	−459 °F	0 K
ice melts	0 °C	32 °F	273 K
human body temperature	37 °C	98.4 °F	310 K
water boils	100 °C	212 °F	373 K

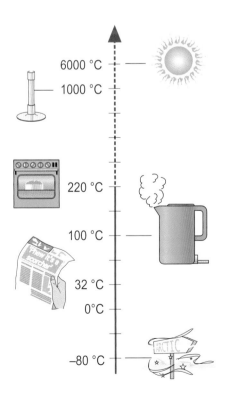

Moving energy

The energy needed to make the temperature of something rise is often called **heat energy**. Another name for this is **thermal energy**.

Heat energy (thermal energy) moves from places with a high temperature to places with a lower temperature if it is able to.

This is why we get heat energy (thermal energy) from the Sun, why a fire heats a room, why food cooks in an oven and why we feel cold when the temperature of the air drops.

Heat energy (thermal energy) is measured in **joules**. A kettle will supply about 2000 joules of heat energy (thermal energy) to the water inside it every second it is on.

When you supply heat energy (thermal energy) to water, the particles move faster. The temperature is a measure of how fast the particles are moving. So, a thermometer is like a speedometer.

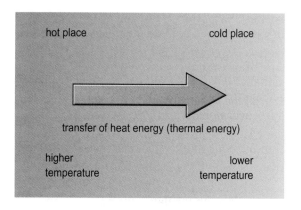

higher temperature → lower temperature
transfer of heat energy (thermal energy)

Question 1

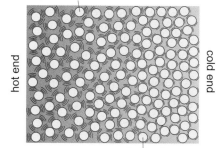

Particles in a solid with one end cold and one end hot.

Conduction

If you put a solid between somewhere hot and somewhere cold, the thermal energy will travel though the solid from the hot region to the cold region. This is called **conduction**.

Thermal energy passes very easily through some solids, especially metals. We say that they are good conductors of heat, or good **thermal conductors**. Very good conductors include copper, aluminium and silver.

The diagram shows how a good conductor is used to cook baked potatoes more quickly than just putting them in the oven.

Question 4

It takes a long time for baked potatoes to cook through to the middle. Using aluminium spikes, they cook through in half the time.

Poor conductors

Some solids, like wood and plastic, do not let the thermal energy travel through them easily. We call them good **thermal insulators** or poor conductors of heat. When hot pans or dishes are put onto a wooden table, it is best to put a mat between the pan and the wood so that the wood does not get scorched or burned by the pan. The mat must be a good insulator.

One of the best insulators is air.

The particles in air are spread out. They bump into each other occasionally as they fly about but, most of the time, there is no connection between them. This means that the particles cannot pass the thermal energy on easily. Air is a poor conductor of heat.

To use air as an insulator, we need to trap it. This idea is used in several different situations.

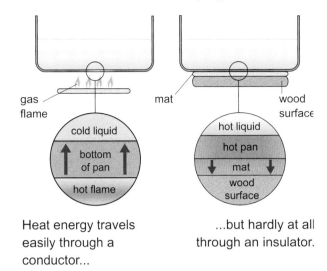

Heat energy travels easily through a conductor...

...but hardly at all through an insulator.

Insulation	How is the air trapped?	Typical uses
foam insulation	as bubbles inside plastic	packaging for fresh food that needs to stay cool
fibre insulation	as bubbles between fibres	knitted clothes, loft insulation
double glazing	as a layer between two panes of glass	windows in houses and offices

Conduction makes some things feel cold

Sometimes, two things at the same temperature feel as if they are at different temperatures when you touch them. A good example is a bike with metal handlebars and a plastic foam saddle.

The metal handlebars feel colder than the seat. Metal is a good conductor. It takes the heat away from your warm hand quickly. It feels cold. The seat is a poor conductor – it does not take the heat away quickly and so it does not feel as cold.

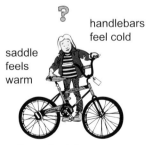

Anna notices that the handlebars of her bicycle feel colder than the saddle.

Anna's science teacher lends her a thermometer. Anna's hand is at 31 °C.

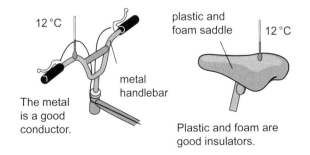

Anna measures the temperature of the handlebars and the saddle. They are both 12 °C.

  Question 6 7 8

You can get heat energy (thermal energy) to move through liquids and gases, but it happens in a different way to the conduction of heat through solids.

Boiling a kettle

Look at the pictures of a kettle.

- The heating element of a kettle heats the water around it.
- The particles in the hot water move faster and move further apart.
- The hot water is less dense than the cold water around it, so the hot water rises up through the cold water.
- Cold water replaces the hot water around the heating element and starts to heat up.
- The water cycles around the kettle until it boils.

This is called **convection**.

Gases and liquids are both fluids. So the same idea about convection applies to the air in a room. Hot air is less dense than cold air, so it rises up from around the wall heater. The cold air moves in to replace it. The cycle of air is known as a **convection current**.

Heat transfers in this way in liquids and gases – because they are fluids, they can flow.

Question 1   2

Using convection currents

Convection currents occur in nature. Dark areas like farm buildings, ploughed fields and tarmac are heated up by the sunlight more than light areas or green fields.

Convection currents rise above them. We call these convection currents thermals. Glider pilots and birds use thermals to gain height.

Question 3

Water next to the heating element gets hotter. This hot water rises.

Colder water then falls down to take its place.

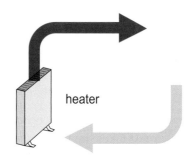

heater

Air next to the heater becomes hotter. This hot air rises. Colder air then falls to take its place.

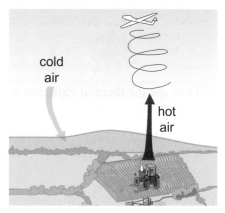

cold air

hot air

Radiation

Heat energy reaches the Earth's surface from the Sun. The energy has travelled across 150 million kilometres of empty space. It does not happen by conduction or convection. There is nothing between the Sun and the Earth to allow conduction or convection to happen. This method of heat transfer is called **radiation** or **thermal radiation**.

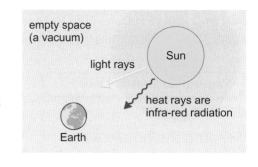

Sometimes, we use the full name: **infra-red radiation**. We say that the Sun radiates heat energy in the same way that it radiates light.

Dark, dull surfaces are good <u>absorbers</u> of infra-red radiation. This means they soak up infra-red radiation well.

Light, shiny surfaces do not absorb infra-red radiation very much. They are good <u>reflectors</u> of radiation.

| Dark clothes make you feel hot on a sunny day. | Astronauts wear shiny suits for space walks. | The tar on roads can melt in the summer sun. | Houses in hot countries are often white. |

Concentrating the radiation from the Sun

If you focus the infra-red radiation from the Sun using a magnifying glass, you concentrate the heat energy enough to set fire to paper.

You can also focus the infra-red radiation using a curved mirror. This idea is used in a solar cooker.

This type of cooker can be used in sunny countries like Africa even if there is an emergency and there is no wood to use as fuel. It is particularly useful for heating impure water above 65 °C for about ten minutes, which kills any bacteria and makes the water safe to drink.

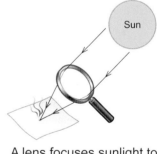

A lens focuses sunlight to a bright spot. The concentrated energy can set fire to paper.

Everything gives off some level of radiation

Everything gives off infra-red radiation. Things at a high temperature give off a lot more radiation than things at a low temperature.

You can use the thermal radiation that is given off to take 'heat' photographs of objects.

Rescue workers use infra-red cameras after earthquakes to see if people are buried under rubble and are still alive.

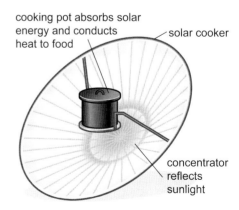

cooking pot absorbs solar energy and conducts heat to food

solar cooker

concentrator reflects sunlight

Question 4 5 6

Check your progress

| You should already know | Outcomes | Keywords |

Keeping the house warm

A house in the UK can cost a lot to keep warm. You can reduce the cost by half if you control the heat loss to the outside air. This diagram shows how much energy you can lose every second from a house on a winter's day.

The total number of joules shown on the diagram would be enough to boil a 1.5 litre kettle of cold water in less than one minute!

You can <u>insulate your loft</u> with layers of glass fibre. Glass fibres trap air. This is a good insulator and reduces heat loss by conduction though the roof.

It costs about £300 to insulate a loft. In a year, you could save about £150 on your heating bills.

<u>Draught excluders</u> only cost a few pounds to fit and they can save about £50 in a year.

<u>Double glazing</u> is expensive. It could take over ten years to save enough on heating bills to cover the cost of double glazing.

Double glazing works by trapping a layer of air between two sheets of glass. The air acts as an insulator.

Double glazing also reduces the level of sound coming in from outside. Many people have double glazing fitted if they live near an airport or on a busy road because it makes it quieter inside the house.

The radiated heat from <u>the back of a radiator</u> can be reflected back into the room by a shiny plastic sheet on the wall.

The walls of most modern houses are made of two layers of brick with plastic foam between them. Foam contains air bubbles and is a very poor conductor of heat. This is called <u>cavity wall insulation</u>.

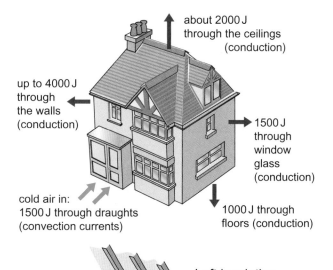

about 2000 J through the ceilings (conduction)

up to 4000 J through the walls (conduction)

1500 J through window glass (conduction)

cold air in: 1500 J through draughts (convection currents)

1000 J through floors (conduction)

Loft insulation

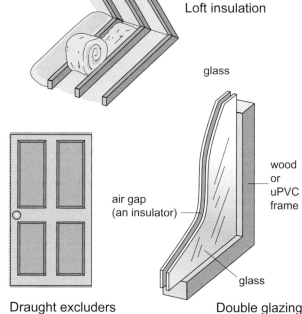

glass

air gap (an insulator)

wood or uPVC frame

glass

Draught excluders

Double glazing

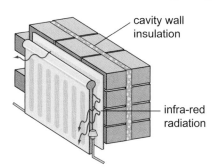

cavity wall insulation

infra-red radiation

Radiator reflector and cavity wall insulation.

Question 1 2

Shiny surfaces are poor radiators of heat

If you fill a black can and a white can with boiling water and leave them to cool for a few minutes, the black can cools more quickly. The diagrams show the temperatures after several minutes of cooling.

The amount of heat radiation given off by something depends not only on how hot it is but also on what its surface is like.

Light-coloured shiny surfaces give off a lot less radiation than dark, dull surfaces. We say that a light, shiny surface is a poor **emitter** of radiation.

At the end of marathon races, runners are at risk of their body temperature falling too much. This is called <u>hypothermia</u>. It happens because they cool quickly in their thin clothes and because of the sweat on their skin.

To prevent hypothermia, runners are wrapped in shiny foil blankets at the end of long races. The shiny surface on the inside of the blanket reflects heat back onto the runner. The shiny surface on the outside reduces the heat lost by the runner.

Question 3

The vacuum flask

A vacuum flask keeps hot things hot and cold things cold. Its walls are designed to prevent heat energy passing through them. It has a double wall with a vacuum in the gap. A vacuum is a space where all or most of the air particles have been sucked out. There are virtually no particles in a vacuum, so conduction and convection cannot happen.

Part	What it does
glass wall	Glass is a poor conductor. It reduces heat loss by conduction.
shiny surfaces	The inside shiny surface does not radiate much heat. The shiny surface on the inside of the outer wall reflects any radiation that does cross the vacuum.
vacuum	Prevents conduction and convection.
stopper	Prevents convection out of the top of the flask.
foam plastic	Reduces conduction through the stopper.

Question 4

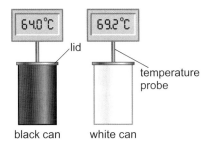

One can is painted black, one white. Otherwise, the two cans are identical.

The silver blanket reflects heat back to the runners' bodies and reduces heat loss by radiation.

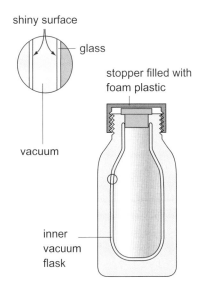

A vacuum flask.

Review your work

Summary ➡

You should already know

Outcomes

Keywords

Gathering evidence

In everyday life, we use our senses to observe things. In science, we use measuring instruments to give us accurate measurements and to extend the range of our senses. For example, you can use a ruler to measure the width of a book but you might use a scale under a microscope to estimate the thickness of a hair.

Sometimes, scientists want to measure many results very rapidly or to take a lot of results over many hours. One convenient way to do this is with a sensor linked to a computer. This type of equipment is also known as a **datalogger**.

Some pupils are using a datalogger to study the temperature of water as it is heated from ice to boiling point.

The diagram shows the experimental set-up at a point part-way through the observations.

There are several advantages of using a datalogger for this experiment.

- The temperature sensor is precise and there is no human error in reading the result it produces.
- The graph showing how the temperature changes as time goes by is plotted as the experiment goes along.
- The computer records the temperature about 60 times every second, so the graph seems like a continuous line.
- The computer stores the results so that they can be used again later without someone having to write them down and then type them in.

We can measure

- manually

- using sensors

- using sensors linked to computers

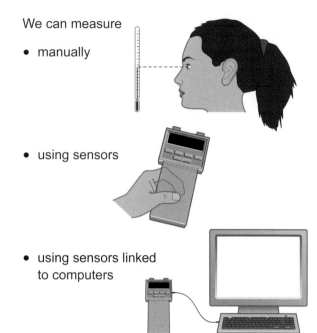

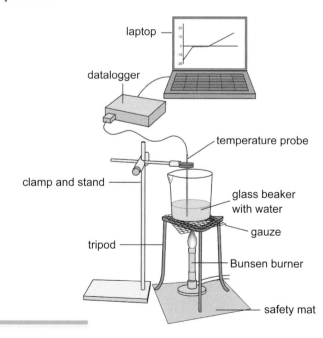

Question 1

Another advantage of a datalogger

The photograph shows a datalogger with three sensors being used to make measurements in a pond. The sensors record different things:

- the amount of oxygen dissolved in the pond water;
- the temperature of the pond water;
- the amount of light falling on the pond water.

The purpose of the experiment was to see whether the level of the oxygen in the pond water was affected by the light falling on the pool and the temperature of the water. In order to carry out the experiment, the scientist had to take readings over a period of 24 hours.

The graph below shows the readings from the temperature sensor over a period of 12 hours.

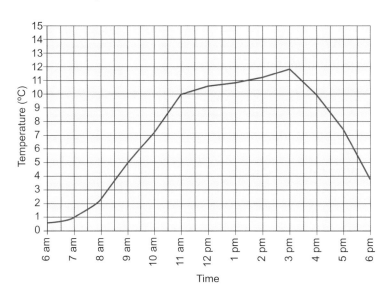

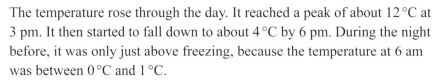

The temperature rose through the day. It reached a peak of about 12 °C at 3 pm. It then started to fall down to about 4 °C by 6 pm. During the night before, it was only just above freezing, because the temperature at 6 am was between 0 °C and 1 °C.

The particular advantages of datalogging in this case were that:

- once the datalogger was set up the experimenters could go away – they didn't have to stay around in the cold and remember to take readings;
- the three readings could all be taken at the same time without needing three people, one for each reading.

 Question 2 **3**

8I Questions

8I.1

1 You can sense how hot or cold a bath for a small child is by dipping your elbow into the water.

   a Suggest a more reliable way of making sure the temperature of the water is not dangerous for the child.

   b Explain why the method you suggest is more reliable.

2 What does the temperature of something tell you?

3 Name <u>two</u> different types of thermometer, and give their advantages and disadvantages.

4 **a** Name <u>two</u> temperature scales used in science.

   b Which of them is used most of the time and is also used in everyday situations?

5 The common type of thermometer used in school laboratories has a temperature range of −10 °C to 110 °C.
Suggest why this is a useful range for the type of science done by school pupils.

8I.2

1 What is the other name for <u>heat energy</u>?

2 **a** When heat energy (thermal energy) moves from one place to another, what is the difference between the two places?

   b Give <u>two</u> examples.

3 **a** What happens to the particles of a substance when heat energy (thermal energy) is transferred to it?

   b What difference could you measure?

4 What is the name for the process by which heat energy passes through a solid?

5 **a** What is meant by a <u>good thermal conductor</u>?

   b Give <u>two</u> examples of materials that are good thermal conductors and an example of <u>one</u> in use.

6 **a** What is meant by a <u>good thermal insulator</u>?

   b Give <u>two</u> examples of materials that are good thermal insulators and an example of <u>one</u> in use.

7 **a** Why is air a poor conductor of heat?

   b How is this idea used to keep things warm?

8 Explain why metal can feel colder than wood even though they are both at the same temperature.

8I.3

1 a What is meant by a <u>convection current</u>?

  b Describe how this transfers heat energy.

2 a In what type of substances can you get convection currents?

  b Why don't convection currents happen in a solid?

3 Give <u>one</u> example of convection currents in nature.

4 a Why must heat from the Sun reach the Earth by a different method than conduction or convection?

  b What is the name for the process that transfers heat energy from the Sun to us?

5 a Describe what a <u>solar cooker</u> is and how it works.

  b In what type of situation is a solar cooker likely to be useful?

6 Describe <u>one</u> use of the fact that all things give off thermal radiation.

8I.4

1 List <u>three</u> different ways of insulating a house and explain how each one works in terms of conduction, convection or radiation.

2 Why might paying for double glazing be a bad idea for someone living in a rented flat for two years?

3 Silver foil blankets are sometimes called <u>survival blankets</u>. Explain how they work.

4 a Describe how a vacuum flask keeps the heat in by referring to conduction, convection and radiation.

  b Why can such a flask be used for keeping things cool instead of keeping things hot?

8I.HSW

1 What are the advantages of using a datalogger to monitor the temperature in the beaker rather than a normal thermometer?

2 Why is a datalogger a useful method for taking readings about the effect of sunlight on the pond?

3 A datalogger is basically a simple computer with one or more sensors attached. It runs on electricity.

Make a list of possible problems you might have to solve if you used a datalogger to monitor conditions at a pond over a period of 48 hours.

You should already know | Outcomes | Keywords

A material that produces a force

Some pieces of rock will **attract** small pieces of iron or steel. This has been known since ancient times. The rock is called <u>lodestone</u>. It is found in many igneous rocks and is a type of iron oxide. Its modern name is <u>magnetite</u>.

If you hang a piece up or float it on water, one end of it points to the north. It was used like this as a **compass** in ancient times.

One piece of lodestone will also attract another piece of lodestone. If you turn one of the pieces round, the pieces of lodestone push each other away. We say that they **repel**.

People discovered that, if you rub a strip of iron with lodestone, the iron will start to behave like the lodestone. Rubbing with lodestone makes iron into a magnet.

You can divide substances into three types.

Some rocks are magnetised. They attract things made of iron or steel.

Magnets	Magnets attract or repel other magnets depending on which way they point. They also attract magnetic materials. They are often made from iron.
Magnetic materials	Magnetic materials are attracted to magnets but do not attract or repel each other.
Non-magnetic materials	These materials are not attracted to magnets.

Magnets.

Most people think that metals are magnetic materials. This is wrong. Contrary to popular belief, of the 80 or so elements that are metals, only three are attracted to a magnet at normal room temperature. These are **cobalt**, **nickel** and **iron**. Steel is a material that contains iron. There are different types of steel. Some are magnetic and some (like high quality stainless steel) are not.

Magnetic materials.

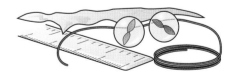

Non-magnetic materials.

Question 1 2 3

Magnetic forces

A strong magnet held on one side of your hand can move a magnetic object on the other side. The magnetic force passes through non-magnetic materials like paper, plastic, paint, skin and bone.

The force between a magnet and another magnet or some magnetic material works through many other materials. We use this idea to keep fridge doors closed. Some people also use magnets to hold written notes onto fridge doors. The small magnets sold to do this are often called <u>fridge magnets</u>.

When a magnet can move freely and is not near other magnets or magnetic materials, it always rests with one end pointing towards the north of the Earth. This end of the magnet is called the **north-seeking pole**, or north pole for short. The other end points towards the south. This is called the **south-seeking pole**, or south pole for short.

The forces produced by a magnet are strongest at its poles.

Objects held on a fridge door by magnets.

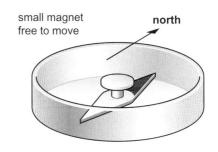

small magnet free to move — north

The only thing that will repel a magnet is another magnet.
If you bring magnets near to each other to see which combination of poles attract and which repel, you get these results.

Poles	Force between poles
north pole near another north pole	repulsion (= pushing apart)
south pole near another south pole	repulsion (= pushing apart)
north pole near a south pole	attraction (= pulling together)

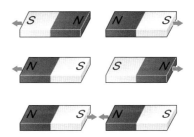

These results produce a basic law.

- Two poles that are different attract each other.
- Two poles that are the same repel each other.

You can use a compass and this law to find out which part of a magnet has which pole.

The diagram shows a bar labelled A at one end and B at the other being brought near to a small compass. In the first diagram, end A attracts the south pole of the compass and it repels the north pole. In the second diagram, end B attracts the north pole of the compass and it repels the south pole of the compass.

This means that end A is a north pole and end B is a south pole.

End A repels the N pole of the compass needle and attracts the S pole.

End B attracts the N pole of the compass needle and repels the S pole.

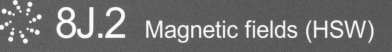

8J.2 Magnetic fields (HSW)

You should already know	Outcomes	Keywords

What is a magnetic field?

A <u>field</u> is an area or open space. The word is usually used to describe an area of land. In science, the term **magnetic field** is used to name an area in which you can detect magnetic forces. The magnetic field around a magnet is the area in which it will attract magnetic materials or push or pull on another magnet.

You can get a picture of magnetic field around a bar magnet by using iron filings or by using small compasses. The diagrams show you how.

small compasses

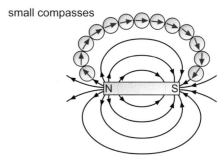

The black lines with arrows show how the compasses point when they are placed there.

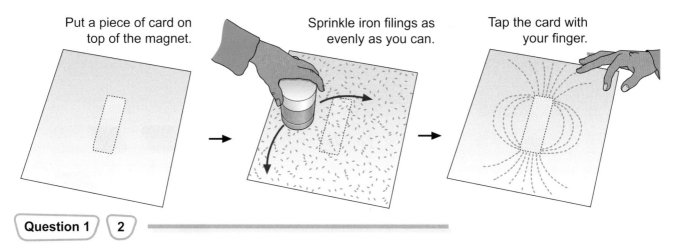

Put a piece of card on top of the magnet. → Sprinkle iron filings as evenly as you can. → Tap the card with your finger.

Question 1 **2**

What do the lines in the magnetic field show?

The lines of the magnetic field show the direction in which a small compass will point if you put it on the line at that point. The lines are sometimes called lines of magnetic force or **magnetic field lines**.

The small arrows on the lines show the direction in which the north pole of the compass points.

Magnets are strongest at their poles. The lines get closer at the poles. Where lines are close together on a map of a magnetic field, the force of magnetism is stronger.

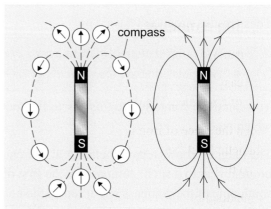

There is a magnetic field all around a magnet.

We can show a magnetic field using lines of magnetic force.

Question 3

The Earth's magnetic field

The needle of a magnetic compass is a small magnet. This magnet is free to turn.

The needle of a magnetic compass comes to rest with one end pointing north and one end pointing south. This happens because the Earth has a magnetic field. The lines of force in the Earth's magnetic field run from the south of the Earth to the north of the Earth.

In 1600, a scientist called William Gilbert published a book called *De Magnete*. The book was written in Latin, so it had a Latin title. The title means *About the Magnet*. This book is important because it was one of the first books written about the results of experiments. It is a book containing facts, not just someone's opinions. In it, Gilbert suggested that the Earth's magnetic field looks like there is a giant bar magnet inside the Earth.

The puzzling thing is that, if there was a large magnet inside the Earth, the pole that would be under the geographic north pole would actually be a magnetic south pole!

A compass does not quite point to the north pole of the Earth. It points to a place near it that we call **magnetic north**. The position of the magnetic north is always changing, very slowly. The table shows how it has moved in the past 400 years or so. It moves because the Earth's magnetism is not actually caused by a big magnet. Some of the Earth's core is a molten liquid that has iron compounds moving about in it. This movement is the main cause of the Earth's magnetic field.

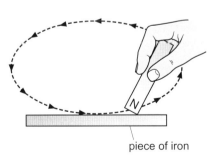

The imaginary magnet that could produce the Earth's magnetic field lines. Its south pole points towards the Arctic and its north pole points towards the Antarctic.

Year	Position of magnetic north
1580	11° east of geographical north
1700	7° west of geographical north
1800	24° west of geographical north
1900	17° west of geographical north
1960	8° west of geographical north

Question 4 **5**

Making a magnet

You can use the field from a magnet to make a piece of iron into a magnet.

One easy way of doing this is to stroke a piece of iron repeatedly with one pole of a magnet. The diagram shows you how.

When the piece of iron is stroked repeatedly in the same direction, the magnetic field from the magnet causes the particles inside the iron to line up so that they produce a magnetic field of their own.

In the diagram, the end of the iron on the right-hand side will become a south pole.

piece of iron

Question 6

Check your progress

You should already know

Outcomes

Keywords

Electricity and magnetism

An electric current has a magnetic field around it. This is a really important thing because, without it, we would not have electric motors and many other things that we take for granted.

This important fact was discovered by accident by a scientist called Hans Christian Oersted in 1819, when he noticed a compass change direction when he turned on an electric current nearby. You can show the effect very easily with a coil of wire. The diagram shows how.

A coil of wire connected to a suitable voltage supply has a magnet field around it when the current flows. It is called an **electromagnet**.

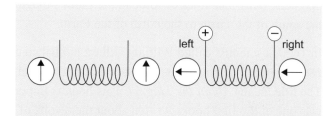

A coil of copper wire does not move a compass needle. The coil is not a magnet.

When a current flows through the coil, the compass needle moves. The coil is just like a magnet.

Question 1 2

Turning on and off

An electromagnet has several advantages over a permanent magnet. You can turn the magnetism on and off by turning the current on and off. You can also change the strength of an electromagnet.

If you drop a packet of paper clips on a carpet with long fibres, they can be quite hard to pick up. If you use a permanent magnet, you have to pick the clips off. With an electromagnet, you can just use the switch.

This idea is used on a much larger scale in scrap yards to move wrecked cars about.

A bar magnet stays magnetised all the time. We call it a permanent magnet.

You have to pick the paper clips off.

The electromagnet in the crane lifts a scrap car.

When the crane driver switches off the current, the car falls.

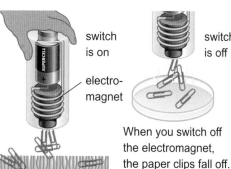

switch is on

electro-magnet

switch is off

When you switch off the electromagnet, the paper clips fall off.

Question 3 4

How do electromagnets work?

Wires carrying an electric current produce a magnetic field around them. If the wire is coiled, the electromagnetic field pattern is similar to that of a bar magnet. If a piece of iron is then placed inside the coil, the iron becomes magnetised. A piece of iron used in this way is called a <u>core</u>. The strength of an electromagnet is increased when an **iron core** is used.

It is important to use 'soft iron' for the core of an electromagnet. Soft iron is iron that does not stay magnetic when the electromagnet is switched off. A piece of steel will still be a magnet when the current is switched off. You can use the coil of an electromagnet to make a permanent magnet from a piece of steel.

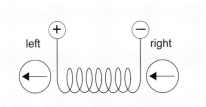

The magnetic field of the iron core adds itself to the magnetic field of the coil.

Reversing the poles

You can change the poles round on an electromagnet by changing the way the electric current flows. The diagrams show what happens when you change over the connections to the power supply.

If you have a power supply that automatically reverses the electric current very quickly, it is called an AC supply.
The magnetism in a coil connected to an AC supply changes so fast that you can use it to make a permanent magnet lose its magnetism altogether. This effect is used in shops to neutralise the security tags on expensive goods so that you can take them out without setting the alarms off.

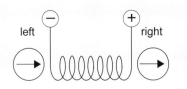

When a current flows through the coil, the comapss needle moves. The coil is just like a magnet.

This is what happens when the current in the coil is reversed.

Question 5 / 6

Changing the strength of an electromagnet

You can change the strength of an electromagnet in three ways.

Way of increasing the strength	Notes
increase the current	Larger electric currents produce stronger magnetic fields. The wires must be thick enough to carry the high current without melting.
have more turns	The more turns you have on an electromagnet, the stronger it is. The problem is that the size of the magnet also increases.
put some soft iron inside	A piece of soft iron inside a coil is called a core. It makes the field stronger. Soft iron is used because it loses its magnetism when the current is switched off.

Question 7

You should already know

Outcomes

Keywords

Separating cans

The steel used to make food cans is a magnetic material. Aluminium, used for drink cans, is not a magnetic material.

An electromagnet can be used to separate a mixture of steel cans from aluminium cans in a recycling plant. The diagram shows how the mixed cans are placed on a conveyer belt and passed under a powerful electromagnet. As the cans pass through, the steel cans are picked off the belt by the electromagnet. The aluminium cans flow off the end, where they are collected.

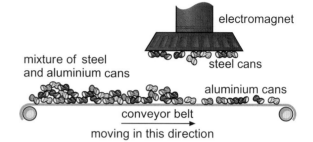

Question 1

Floating trains

Trains that run on one rail are called <u>monorail</u> trains. They are used for public transport in Tokyo in Japan and Seattle in the USA. One way to build a monorail uses magnets to make the train float above the rail. This makes the friction very low. The train uses less energy than a train running on wheels.

The diagram shows a design in which the magnets are attracted to the rail and this force lifts the train off the rail.

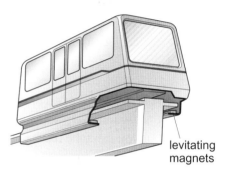

Question 2

Recording information

Magnetic tape can be used to store information. The tape contains many tiny magnetic particles. The information is stored by magnetising the particles in different patterns.

This technology has been used to record music, to store computer data and to hold information on credit and debit cards.

Magnetic tape is still common in some car parks for the tickets. The magnetic strip on the ticket records the time you arrive at the car park. When you put it in the pay machine, the machine reads the time and records that you have paid. The ticket raises the barrier on the way out. If you put your ticket in a bag with a magnetic catch, the ticket might fail to work!

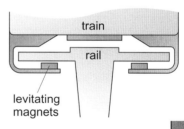

When the information is recorded on the magnetic strip, the magnetic particles line up into a pattern.

Question 3

Bells

Some bells use electromagnets. The diagram shows a typical electric bell circuit. The iron core with the coils around it is an electromagnet. When the switch is pressed, a cycle of events take place.

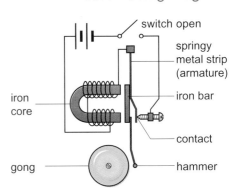

- When the switch is pressed, the current flows around the circuit.
- The electromagnet is turned on.
- The iron bar is attracted to the iron core of the electromagnet and the hammer hits the gong.
- When the iron bar moves to the left, the contact at the back of it is broken.
- The current stops flowing and the electromagnet turns off.
- The iron bar is no longer attracted to the electromagnet and the spring moves it back.
- The contact is made again and the cycle starts once more with current flowing around the circuit.

Question 4

Relays

The **relay** is a very important use of an electromagnet. A relay is a switch based on an electromagnet that lets one current turn on another.

The diagram shows how a pressure switch will turn on an electromagnet in a relay. The iron in the relay moves and makes the contact in the second circuit to light the bulb.

Car starter motors use relays. A small current flows in one circuit when the ignition key is turned. This makes a relay switch on a very large current to the starter motor.

The relay is a way for a small safe current to switch on a large dangerous one.

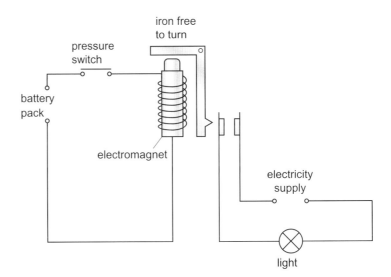

This circuit controls a light that switches on if someone steps on the pressure switch.

Question 5

Review your work

Summary ➡

You should already know

Outcomes

Keywords

Gathering data

Scientists record and analyse data from a wide range of sources. Sometimes, these sources are their own experiments – these are examples of **primary sources**. Sometimes, they get results from other people, written reports, books or the Internet – these are called **secondary sources**.

> **Remember**
>
> Scientists use data to provide evidence for scientific explanations.

Wherever the data comes from, it can also be classed as either **qualitative** or **quantitative**.

Qualitative	the data is in the form of words or pictures
Quantitative	the data is in the form of numbers

The diagram shows an investigation into how strong two magnets are. The magnet that can hold the most paper clips in a chain will be the strongest.

This is the data from the experiment.

Magnet	Strength measurement
bar magnet	four paper clips
horseshoe magnet	seven paper clips

The strength measurement is an example of <u>quantitative</u> data.

If you tested some different materials to see whether they were magnetic, you might get results like this.

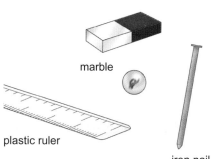

Object	Observation
plastic ruler	not attracted to a magnet – not magnetic
marble	not attracted to a magnet – not magnetic
iron nail	attracted to a magnet – magnetic

marble

plastic ruler

iron nail

These are examples of <u>qualitative</u> data.

Question 1 2

Investigations with magnets

The aim of this investigation is to find out whether the magnetic force will pass through different thicknesses of paper.

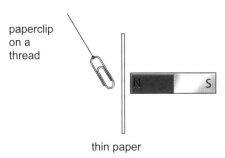

paperclip on a thread

thin paper

Different thicknesses of paper are placed between the magnet and the clip. The angle between the thread and the vertical is a measurement of the magnetic force.

A pupil who did the investigation produced these results.

Thickness of paper	Angle of thread from vertical
thin	31°
thicker	31°
very thick	31°

Question 3 **4**

Investigating the strength of an electromagnet

A similar idea can be used to investigate the strength of an electromagnet.

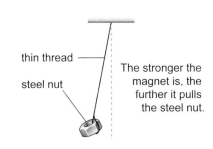

thin thread

steel nut

The stronger the magnet is, the further it pulls the steel nut.

The electromagnet attracts the steel nut. You can use the angle the thread makes with the vertical as a measure of how strong the magnet is.

There are three ways of changing the strength of an electromagnet. So we need three investigations to test the strength. The diagrams show part of the experimental set-up for each investigation.

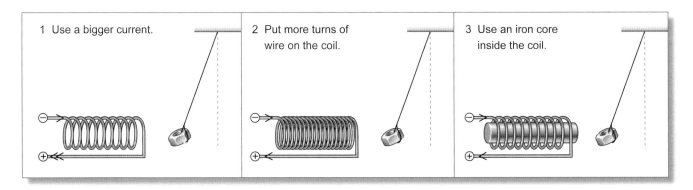

1 Use a bigger current.

2 Put more turns of wire on the coil.

3 Use an iron core inside the coil.

To get <u>quantitative</u> data, you would also need:

- an ammeter to measure the size of the current flowing in the electromagnet;
- a protractor and plumb line to measure the angle between the thin thread and the vertical.

Question 5 **6**

8J.1

1   What things does a lodestone do that make it different from pieces of rock that do not contain magnetite?

2   **a**   What things are attracted to magnets?

    b   Comment on this statement.
       'Magnets attract metal objects.'

3   You have two small bars of metal that are attracted to each other. You know that one of them is a magnet.
    What test could you do to find out whether they are both magnets? Explain your answer.

4   What is a compass and what does it do?

5   **a**   Why does a strip of plastic containing magnets provides a better way of closing a fridge door than an ordinary catch?

    b   Plastic would be a cheaper material than steel for making the doorframe for a fridge. Why is steel used instead of plastic?

6   Describe the different combinations of poles that cause attraction and repulsion between magnets.

7   A piece of metal is brought near to a compass and the compass needle moves towards the metal.

    a   What can you conclude about the metal?

    b   What test would you have to do to conclude that the metal was a magnet?

    Explain your answer.

8J.2

1   What is meant by the term <u>magnetic field</u>?

2   How can you get a picture of the magnetic field around a magnet?

3   What do the lines of magnetic force show, and how can you tell where the field is the strongest?

4   Why does a compass point to the north of the Earth?

5   Why does the Earth have a magnetic field?

6   **a**   Describe how you can make a magnet.

    b   How could you tell which pole was which on the magnet you make?

8J.3

1 How could you use a compass to test whether a wire had a constant electric current flowing through it? Explain your answer.

2 What is an electromagnet?

3 Give two advantages of an electromagnet over a magnet made from a piece of metal.

4 **a** Why is an electromagnet useful on a crane in a scrap yard?

    b Is it useful for every possible type of car?
    Give a reason for your answer.

5 Why do some electromagnets have a core of soft iron?

6 What happens if you reverse the current in an electromagnet?

7 Describe how the strength of an electromagnet can be changed.

8J.4

1 Which type of can is collected by the electromagnet in a magnetic separator? Give a reason for your answer.

2 Describe how magnets can be used to reduce friction in a monorail train.

3 How can magnetism be used to store information?

4 Describe the operation of an electric bell.

5 What does a relay do? Explain how an electromagnet operates in a relay.

8J.HSW

1 **a** What is the difference between primary sources and secondary sources?

    b Give one example of each type.

2 **a** What is the difference between quantitative data and qualitative data?

    b Give one example of each type.

3 What are the different types of data in the pupil's experiment to test whether the magnetic force passes through paper?

4 **a** How could the pupil have changed the experiment to make all the observations quantitative?

    b Do you think that would have made the experiment any better?

5 For each experiment shown in the diagram, describe:

    a what you would change (the independent variable);

    b what you would measure (the dependent variable);

    c what you would keep the same (control variables).

    For each variable, state whether it is quantitative or qualitative.

6 Describe how you would carry out one of the three experiments, including how you would use the protractor and plumb line to measure the angle of the thread.

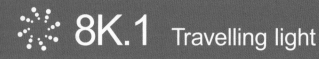

You should already know | Outcomes | Keywords

Where does light come from?

A **light source** is anything that produces light. The Sun is our main light source but, since prehistoric times, humans have used other light sources to help them see when it is dark.

Electric light sources can be switched on and off instantly. Electric lights do not have flames in them. There is less risk of starting a fire. Electricity is more convenient and safer than candles and oil lamps.

Some light sources.

Light travels in straight lines

The demonstration shows that light travels in straight lines. This is why we use straight lines with arrows to represent light. We call each line a **ray**. A light ray shows the path that the light follows. A diagram with rays to show what light does is called a <u>ray diagram</u>.

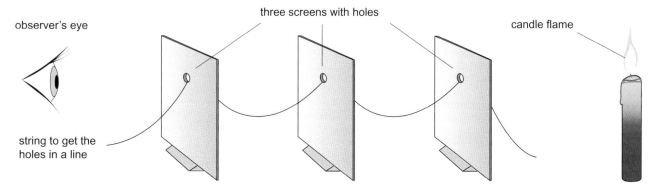

observer's eye

three screens with holes

candle flame

string to get the holes in a line

If you pull the string tight, the holes move into line and you can see the candle flame.

The ray diagram shows how a torch and a pencil can be used to make a shadow. The light cannot go through the pencil. Because light travels in straight lines, it cannot go round the pencil. That is why the pencil casts a shadow when it is put in front of the torch.

The rays from the torch are spreading out. The light from the Sun is spreading out all over space. Because the Earth is so far away from the Sun, the Sun's light rays reach us in a parallel beam.

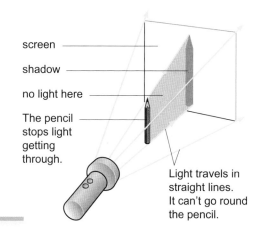

screen

shadow

no light here

The pencil stops light getting through.

Light travels in straight lines. It can't go round the pencil.

Question 1 / 2

The speed of light

If you go to watch a cricket match, you see the ball being hit but you hear the sound a short time later. This happens because light travels at an incredibly high speed. It seems to reach you straight away. Sound travels about a million times slower than light. Over a distance of more than about 50 metres, you see things before you hear them.

This effect can be used to estimate how far away a thunderstorm is.

Thunder is the sound produced by a bolt of lightning. If a thunderstorm is in the distance, you see the lightning a long time before you hear the thunder. However, the speed of light is so high that you see the lightning almost instantly. The sound takes about three seconds to travel one kilometre.

If you count the seconds between seeing the lightning flash and hearing the thunder, the distance to the storm is about one kilometre for every three seconds you count.

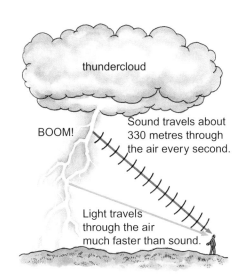

thundercloud

BOOM!

Sound travels about 330 metres through the air every second.

Light travels through the air much faster than sound.

Question 3

What is the speed of light?

The first attempt to measure how fast light travels was by the Italian scientist Galileo Galilei in 1600. He tried uncovering a lantern and timing how long the light took to travel a few miles to another person. His idea did not work. The speed of light was too high to measure by his method.

Scientists made the first really accurate measurements of the speed of light about 150 years ago using a spinning mirror. We now know that light travels 300 000 000 metres in one second.

It is almost impossible to imagine what a speed of 300 000 000 m/s means.

Mama mia! I did not expect that! His light came on straight away. The speed of light is too high for me to measure.

Distance	Time for light to travel that distance
from a lamp to the door of a room (about 3 m)	one hundred-millionth of a second
from a lighthouse to a ship 30 km away	one ten-thousandth of a second
from the Sun to the Earth (150 000 000 km)	about 500 seconds (8 minutes and 20 seconds)
from the nearest star to us (about 40 400 000 000 000 km)	about 135 000 000 seconds (about 4.25 years)
from the edge of the observable universe to us (about 100 000 000 000 000 000 000 000 km)	about 10 000 million years

Question 4 **5**

| You should already know | Outcomes | Keywords |

What happens when light hits an object?

When light hits something it can do one of three things:

- go through (be **transmitted**);
- bounce back (be **reflected**);
- stay inside and heat up the object (be **absorbed**).

Some substances let almost all of the light go straight through them. Glass, water, air and some types of plastic are good examples. We say that these substances are **transparent**.

Even transparent substances absorb light a little bit but the amount is usually so small that we can ignore it. Sometimes, there is a combination of reflection, transmission and absorption. If enough light goes through for you to see clearly through the substance we still say that it is transparent.

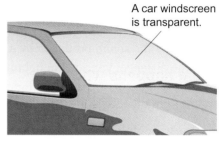

A car windscreen is transparent.

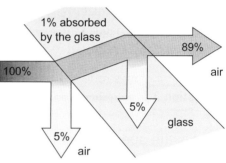

Even with transparent glass, 5% of light can reflect at each surface. Only 89% of light gets through.

| Question 1 | 2 |

Translucent substances

Sometimes, you want to let the <u>light</u> through but you do not want anyone to be able to <u>see</u> through. Substances that let light through but do not let you see a clear image through them are called **translucent** substances. Examples of translucent substances in use are:

- frosted glass in a bathroom window;
- sheets of white cotton used as sun blinds;
- the glass bulb of a 'pearl' lamp.

Translucent substances scatter light in all directions as it passes through so that you cannot see a clear image through them. Clouds are translucent. The Sun's light is scattered when it comes through them. That is why you do not get shadows on a cloudy day even though it is still light.

frosted glass

cotton blind

Some light gets through, but you can't see through the frosted window or the blind.

Light from Sun. Clouds reflect some light.

Some light gets through. The light scatters in all directions.

| Question 3 |

Opaque substances

Some substances stop light going through them. We say that a substance that stops light is **opaque**. Metal and wood are opaque substances. Some types of plastic are also opaque.

Opaque substances are used for blackout blinds and, in photography, to prevent light reaching light-sensitive film.

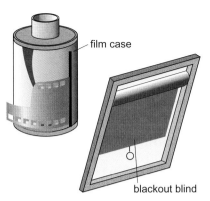

film case

blackout blind

You must use an opaque substance for the case of a photographic film or the light will spoil it. The windows in a roof can be fitted with opaque blinds to shut sunlight out completely.

Question 4

What happens when light hits a surface?

When light hits a surface, some of it bounces off. We say that it is <u>reflected</u>.

In the case of transparent glass, only a very tiny amount is reflected. In the case of an opaque substance, almost all of it can be reflected. How much light is reflected can depend on the colour of the surface.

Pale or white things reflect most of the light that falls on them. That is why these surfaces look pale or white.

Black and dark things absorb most of the light that falls on them. That is why they look black or dark.

You see an object because the light coming from it enters your eye.

For objects that give out light, like light bulbs, that usually means that the light has travelled in a straight line from them to your eye.

For objects that do not give out light, you see them when light reflects off them into your eye.

If an object reflects very little light, it can be hard to see. This is why birds sometimes crash into the windows of houses.

White things and pale things reflect most of the light that falls on them.

Black things and dark things reflect very little of the light that falls on them. They absorb most of the light.

Some things give out their own light.

light from Sun

Sun

Moon

We can see other things because they reflect light.

Objects that give out light are called **luminous** objects.

Objects that do not give out light are called **non-luminous** objects.

Question 5 **6**

The only luminous object in this room is the light bulb. When it is not on, none of the objects in the room can be seen.

You should already know ⟩ ⟨ Outcomes ⟩ ⟨ Keywords ⟩

How different surfaces reflect light

The diagram shows a spotlight shining on a picture. The picture has a surface that has a lot of very tiny bumps on it. The bumps mean the light that hits the picture reflects in all directions.

A shiny surface is one that is very smooth. When light reflects off a shiny surface, it is not scattered in all directions. This means you can see a clear reflection in the surface.

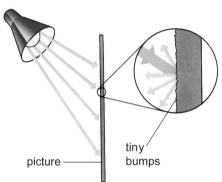

The picture has a bumpy surface. So it reflects light in all directions.

mirror (glass with silvered back)

polished metal spoon

You can see your own reflection in these.

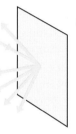

A piece of paper scatters light in all directions.

A mirror reflects all the light in the same direction.

How a mirror reflects light

A mirror reflects light so that it bounces off at the <u>same</u> angle as it hit the mirror with.

We measure the angle of the light hitting and leaving the mirror from a reference line called a **normal**. The normal is a line drawn at 90° to the surface of the mirror.

The ray of light hitting the mirror is called the <u>incident ray</u>. The angle between it and the normal is called the **angle of incidence**.

The ray of light reflecting off the mirror is called the <u>reflected ray</u>. The angle between it and the normal is called the **angle of reflection**.

When light reflects off a mirror, the angle of incidence equals the angle of reflection.

mirror

incident ray (light coming in)

A

angle of incidence

angle of reflection — normal

B

reflected ray (light going out)

Angle A and angle B are equal. The mirror reflects a beam at the same angle as it strikes the mirror.

⟨ Question 1 ⟩ ⟨ 2 ⟩

Looking in a mirror

A flat mirror is also known as a <u>plane</u> mirror. When you look into a plane mirror you see an **image** of your face. We call the thing that the light comes from the **object**. So, here, your face is the object.

Because of the way light reflects off a flat mirror, the image of your face follows certain rules.

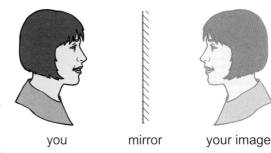

you   mirror   your image

- The image is the same size as the object – your face does not look bigger or smaller.
- Your reflection looks as though it is as far into the mirror as your face is in front of the mirror.
- The image is the opposite way around to the object.

> **Question 3**

Using mirrors

If you want to see over the top of something, you can use two mirrors in a tube. This is called a **periscope**.

The light enters the periscope, reflects off the first mirror at the top and travels down to the bottom mirror, where the light is reflected into your eye. Periscopes are used for seeing over crowds, observing wildlife from behind walls and, in submarines, for looking out over the surface of the sea.

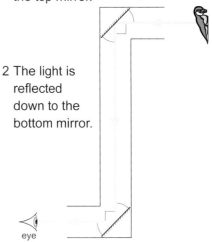

1 Light from the woodpecker hits the top mirror.

2 The light is reflected down to the bottom mirror.

3 It is then reflected into your eye, so you see the woodpecker.

seeing over a crowd

battleship

submarine

birdwatcher

woodpecker

Mirrors are also used at dangerous junctions and bends to help drivers see whether another car is coming. In this picture, the driver of the blue car can just see the front of the yellow car along a direct line of sight. The driver can see the red car in the mirror.

Because the light takes the same path in the opposite direction, the driver of the red car can see that there is a blue car waiting at the junction.

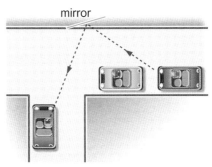

mirror

Mirrors are sometimes used to help drivers see around corners.

> **Question 4**

> **Check your progress**

You should already know | Outcomes | Keywords

Changing direction

You can change the direction of a ray of light by bouncing it off a mirror. You can also change its direction by shining it into a different transparent substance. When you shine a ray of light at an angle from one substance into another, it changes its direction. When light bends like this, the effect is called **refraction** ('refraction' means 'bending'). We say that the light has been <u>refracted</u>. (The dotted line drawn on the diagrams is the normal.)

Refraction works in both directions.

- If you shine a ray of light <u>into</u> a transparent substance like water or glass from the air, it bends <u>towards</u> the normal.
- If you shine a ray of light <u>out of</u> a transparent substance like water or glass into the air, it bends <u>away from</u> the normal.
- If you shine it along the normal in any direction, it doesn't bend at all.

The angle at which the light shines into the new substance affects the amount of refraction.

- When there is a large angle between the light ray and the normal, the refraction (the bending) is large.
- When a light ray travels along the normal, there is no refraction.

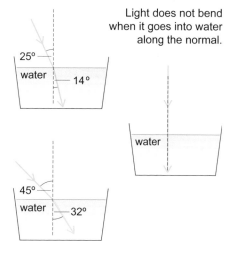

Light does not bend when it goes into glass along the normal.

Light bends towards the normal when it goes into glass or water.

Light does not bend when it goes into water along the normal.

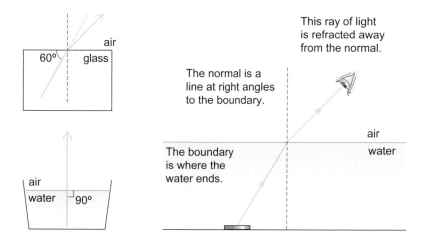

The normal is a line at right angles to the boundary.

This ray of light is refracted away from the normal.

The boundary is where the water ends.

Question 1 2 3 4

Seeing around corners

You can use refraction to see round corners. In the first picture, Kris cannot see the coin because the light ray that travels past the edge of the metal can does not enter his eye.

In the second picture, his friend Sam has added some water while Kris keeps his head still. The coin comes into view because the light ray from it is refracted (bent) as it comes out of the water.

Kris can see the coin now because the light from it enters his eye.

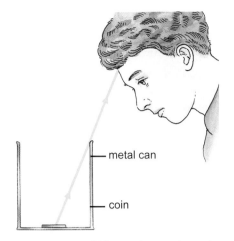

metal can

coin

Kris can't see the coin

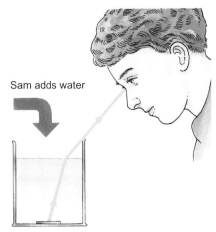

Sam adds water

Now Kris can see the coin

Shallow water

When you look into water, refraction makes it look shallower than it really is. This picture shows what happens. The image of the coin does not appear to be as deep as the coin itself is. It seems to be closer to the surface.

This effect can be dangerous for people who cannot swim and who do not know that water seems shallower than it really is. A pool that is 2 m deep will appear to be only 1.5 m deep because of the refraction effect.

The same effect can be seen in other situations.

- A straight ruler looks bent when you put it into water.
- A swimmer looks shorter when standing under the water in a pool.
- A fish sees a fly in a different position to where it actually is.

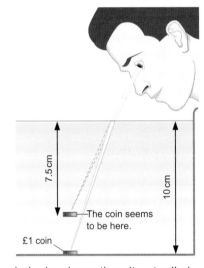

7.5 cm

10 cm

The coin seems to be here.

£1 coin

The coin looks closer than it actually is.

This ruler is straight.

But if you dip it into water, it looks bent.

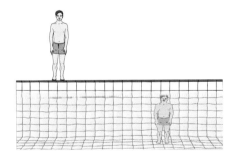

The boy looks shorter in water because light is refracted as it goes from water to air.

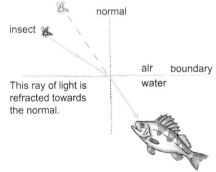

normal

insect

air   boundary

water

This ray of light is refracted towards the normal.

To the fish, the fly seems higher up than it actually is.

Question 5

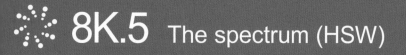

| You should already know | Outcomes | Keywords |

Newton's discovery

If you go to Woolsthorpe Manor in Lincolnshire, you can see a small room with a piece of glass called a **prism** set up to catch the Sun's rays coming through a hole in a window shutter. The glass prism splits the sunlight into a rainbow of colours on the wall.

The room is where Isaac Newton first worked out that white light is made up of colours, on 21st August 1665.

The prism used to split white light into its colours has a triangular cross section. You get exactly the same effect with a prism made from plastic as you do with one made from glass.

Because of its shape, the prism refracts the light twice in the same direction. This splits white light up into the colours it is made from. The diagram shows you what happens.

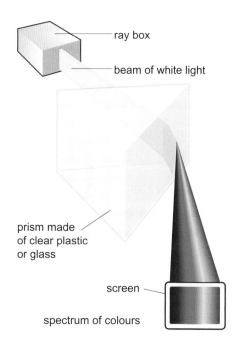

ray box

beam of white light

prism made of clear plastic or glass

screen

spectrum of colours

The spectrum

The rainbow of colours is called a **spectrum**. If you look at a spectrum, you will see that the colours gradually blend from one to the other, from a deep red at one end to a deep violet at the other.

One way to remember the order of the colours is to use this phrase:

> Richard Of York Gave Battle In Vain.

Each capital letter stands for a colour.

Word	Richard	Of	York	Gave	Battle	In	Vain
Colour	red	orange	yellow	green	blue	indigo	violet

The seven-word phrase is just a way of remembering the order.
It is important to remember that there are not actually any separate bands of colour in a spectrum, just a gradual change of shade.

 Question 1 2 ─────────────────

Rainbows

Sometimes, you can see a rainbow when the Sun is shining and it is raining at the same time.

The raindrops work in a similar way to tiny prisms in the sunlight even though they are spherical and not triangular.

If you are going to see a rainbow, you have to be in the right position. The angles have to be correct between the Sun, the rain and your eyes.

- You need to stand with your back to the sunlight.
- The angle between the direction of the sunlight and your line of sight to the raindrops must be about 42°.

When you see a rainbow, red appears at the top and violet appears at the bottom.

The white sunlight enters the top of the raindrops and splits into a spectrum. Each colour emerges at a different angle. You see red light emerging from the higher raindrops and violet emerging from the lower ones. The spectrum is formed by the colours coming out of the raindrops in between.

You can make an artificial rainbow with a mist of drops from a garden hose.

Drops of rain can be split into all the colours of the rainbow.

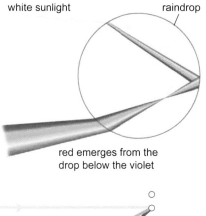

white sunlight   raindrop

red emerges from the drop below the violet

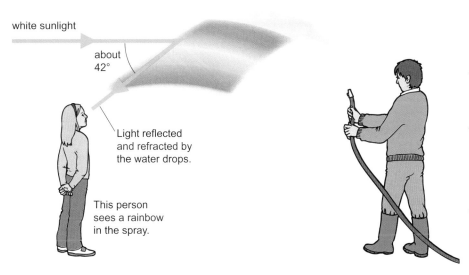

white sunlight

about 42°

Light reflected and refracted by the water drops.

This person sees a rainbow in the spray.

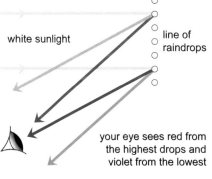

white sunlight

line of raindrops

your eye sees red from the highest drops and violet from the lowest

Another way of splitting white light into colours is to look at the Sun's reflection on the shiny side of a CD while tilting the CD. You can see some interesting rainbow patterns.

 Question 3 / 4

Review your work

Summary ➡

You should already know

Outcomes

Keywords

Using light

Light travels incredibly fast.

White light is made up from all the colours of the spectrum mixed together. We get most of our information about the world by using light – mainly by looking at things.

The pictures show some of the ways we use light. All these are examples of how scientific ideas have been applied to bring about **technological developments**. Some of them have happened within the past hundred years – for example, the first traffic lights were installed in London in 1932.

Question 1 / 2

Laser light

Laser light is a very pure type of light. This light was first produced using a ruby crystal in 1960. Since then, a lot of development has happened by many scientists sharing ideas between them. This is an example of scientists working together.

Laser light can be made to carry so much energy that it will cut steel. It can also be made so that it does not carry so much energy and is safe to use in everyday situations. For example:

- to scan bar codes in supermarkets;
- to read the information on CDs and DVDs.

Laser light is reflected from the white parts of the bar code and absorbed by the black bars. A sensor detects the reflected light pattern as the code is scanned. The pattern depends on the widths of the bars. A computer translates the pattern into a number that identifies the product.

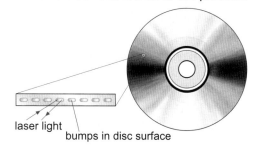

laser light

bumps in disc surface

A CD player works in a similar way. A pattern of microscopic bumps in the disc reflect the laser beam as the disc spins.

Question 3

Optical fibres

In 1955 a scientist worked out that, if you had a very fine fibre that was transparent, you could send light down it and the light would not escape out of the sides of the fibre. This is a very useful idea. It works in a similar way to a pipe carrying sound by it reflecting off the sides.

The use of optical fibres in medicine is an example of how applying a scientific idea can bring about changes in people's lives. It is also an example of people sharing developments between different areas, in this case physics and medicine. This is called **collaboration**.

The use of optical fibres means that medical staff can see what is happening inside patients without cutting them open. This is done using a group of optical fibres called an <u>endoscope</u>. The diagrams show how it works.

Optical fibres are also used so that surgeons can carry out <u>keyhole surgery</u>. This is a lot safer than major surgery because it causes less damage to the patient.

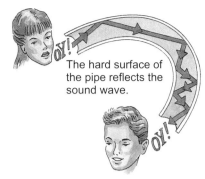

The hard surface of the pipe reflects the sound wave.

Sound waves travelling through a pipe.

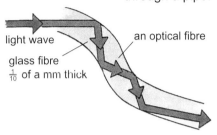

light wave

glass fibre $\frac{1}{10}$ of a mm thick

an optical fibre

Light waves travelling through an optical fibre.

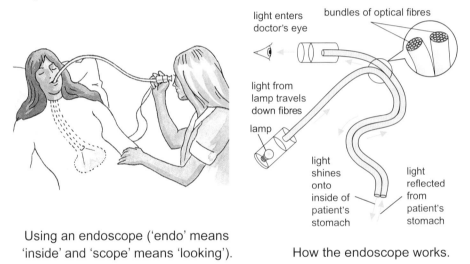

Using an endoscope ('endo' means 'inside' and 'scope' means 'looking').

light enters doctor's eye

bundles of optical fibres

light from lamp travels down fibres

lamp

light shines onto inside of patient's stomach

light reflected from patient's stomach

How the endoscope works.

Question 4 **5**

Safety

Scientists always have to assess the risk of what they do in the laboratory and the workplace. When a scientific idea is used in everyday life, the same thing applies. You can see **hazard** warnings on equipment such as CD players, like the one shown.

Laser light is not the only type of light that can be dangerous. Any very bright light can damage your eyes. If people work in situations where bright light is a hazard, they have to wear masks or goggles with dark filters to protect their eyes.

Question 6

DANGER

LASER RADIATION - AVOID DIRECT EYE EXPOSURE

Laser beams must never be directed into or towards eyes.

A welding torch makes metal white hot. The operator must use a mask with a dark filter to protect her eyes from the high intensity light.

8K.1

1 How can you show that light travels in straight lines?

2 How can the idea of light rays explain how a shadow forms?

3 Describe an effect that shows that light travels faster than sound.

4 Why did early attempts to measure the speed of light fail?

5 In astronomy, very large distances are measured in light years. A light year is the distance light travels in a year.

If light travels 300 000 000 metres every second, work out how far it travels in a year. Show how you worked out your answer.

8K.2

1 What can happen to light when it hits a substance?

2 **a** What is meant by a <u>transparent</u> substance?

    b Give some examples of where transparent substances are used, with reasons.

3 **a** What is meant by a <u>translucent</u> substance?

    b Give some examples of where translucent substances are used, with reasons.

4 **a** What is meant by an <u>opaque</u> substance?

    b Give some examples of where opaque substances are used, with reasons.

5 What is the difference between the way light things and dark things reflect light?

6 **a** What is the difference between a luminous object and a non-luminous object?

    b What has to happen for you to see a non-luminous object?

8K.3

1 Explain what is meant by these terms when light reflects off a plane mirror.

    a angle of incidence

    b angle of reflection

    c normal

2 **a** What is the law that connects the angle of incidence and the angle of reflection when light reflects off a plane mirror?

    b How could you test this law?

3 What can be said about the image that is formed in a plane mirror in relation to the object?

4 Give <u>two</u> examples of the use of plane mirrors in everyday life.

8K.4

1. What is meant by <u>refraction</u> and when does it happen?

2. Describe the bending of light when it <u>goes into</u> a substance like water or glass from the air.

3. Describe the bending of light when it <u>emerges from</u> a substance like water or glass into the air.

4. What is the only angle that light can travel along that will cause no bending?

5. Describe <u>three</u> everyday effects of refraction.

8K.5

1. What is a triangular prism and how is it used to show that white light can be split into colours?

2. a What are the <u>seven</u> colours that make up white light?

   b What is the name for them all together?

3. a What do you have to do to see a rainbow?

   b Whereabouts in a rainbow do the different colours of the spectrum appear?

4. Give <u>two</u> other examples of where you can see a spectrum (apart from when it is raining and sunny at the same time, and by using a prism).

8K.HSW

1. Give <u>three</u> examples of how technological developments in the use of light have changed the way people behave.

2. In 2003, Drachten (a town in Holland) stopped using its traffic lights and the number of road accidents fell. In September 2007 the London borough of Kensington and Chelsea announced that it had plans to do the same thing in some streets.

   a Suggest how traffic lights change motorists' behaviour.

   b Why might removing traffic lights reduce the number of accidents?

   c Use the Internet to research the development of traffic lights from 1868 to the present day.

3. a Find out what the letters of the word 'laser' stand for.

   b Find out how laser light is used to read a CD.

4. Optical fibres are used in communication systems. Find out how an optical fibre can be use to replace a metal wire in a telephone system.

5. Laser light can be used to change the shape of a person's eye so that they do not need to wear glasses or contact lenses. This is sometimes called <u>laser eye treatment</u>.

   Use the Internet to find out what this is. Make a list of points for it and against it.

6. Find out which part of the eye is likely to be damaged if high energy light like laser light enters your eye.

8L.1 Making different sounds (HSW)

You should already know | Outcomes | Keywords

What causes sound?

Many different things make sounds. They all have one thing in common. They **vibrate**.

Sounds are caused by **vibrations**.

A vibration is a fast backwards-and-forwards movement that repeats many times. If you put your fingers against your throat as you speak then you will feel the vibrations.

Musical instruments all have some way of making vibrations. These make the sounds and notes that the musician needs. A saxophone has a reed in the mouthpiece that vibrates when it is blown. The moving reed makes the air inside the tube of the instrument vibrate and produce a note.

A loudspeaker makes a sound when its paper cone vibrates backwards and forwards.

You can hear the washing machine because it is vibrating.

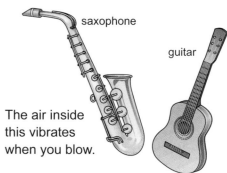

saxophone

guitar

The air inside this vibrates when you blow.

The strings vibrate when you pluck them.

Question 1 | 2

Different sounds

There are lots of different sounds. One way in which sounds can be different is in how loud they are. We refer to this as their **loudness**.

The loudness of a sound you hear depends on three things:

- how big the vibration is that produces the sound;
- how far away you are from the sound;
- if there is anything between you and the sound.

The photographs show two situations in which you make the sound louder by making the vibrations larger.

Turning up the volume produces a bigger vibration in the loudspeaker.

Hitting the drum harder produces a bigger vibration.

Question 3

What is amplitude?

Loud sounds are made by vibrations that are large. We say that the vibrations have a large **amplitude**. The amplitude of a vibration is how far something moves from its rest position when it is moving backwards and forwards.

When the sound is loud, the air particles vibrate a lot; they have a large amplitude. When the sound is quiet, the air particles only vibrate a little bit; they have a small amplitude.

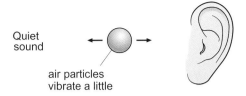

Quiet sound — air particles vibrate a little

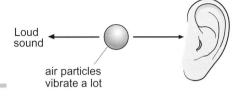

Loud sound — air particles vibrate a lot

> **Question 4**

What is pitch?

Sounds can be high or low. A motorbike engine ticking over gives out a sound with a low pitch. A cat complaining about something gives out a high-pitched sound!

The pitch depends on <u>how many</u> vibrations the source of the sound produces in a second. The number of vibrations per second that the source of sound makes is called its **frequency**.

- Frequency is measured in **hertz** (symbol Hz).
- A frequency of 1 Hz means that there is one vibration per second.
- 2000 Hz means that there are 2000 vibrations per second.

Large objects usually produce lower frequencies than smaller objects because large objects usually vibrate more slowly. The picture shows a violin and a cello. If both instruments are played in the same way then the note from the violin will be a lot higher.

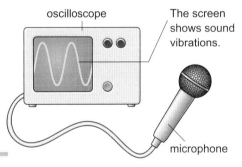

oscilloscope

The screen shows sound vibrations.

microphone

> **Question 5** **6**

Looking at pitch and amplitude

If you connect a microphone to an oscilloscope, you can get a picture of a sound. The microphone changes the sounds into an electrical signal, and the oscilloscope shows this electrical signal as a graph.

The <u>height</u> of the oscilloscope signal shows the <u>amplitude</u> of the sound.

<u>How often</u> the wave goes up and down gives the <u>frequency</u> of the vibration.

Notice that we measure the amplitude of a wave from the mid-point to its highest point.

This is the amplitude of the wave.

Quiet sound.

Loud sound.

High-pitched sound.

Low-pitched sound.

> **Question 7**

You should already know | Outcomes | Keywords

How sound travels from a loudspeaker

When a loudspeaker produces a sound, its cone vibrates backwards and forwards. This makes the air particles in front of it move backwards and forwards at the same frequency. These air particles push the next layer of air particles and make them vibrate, and so on. This vibration passing from air particle to air particle is called a <u>sound wave</u>.

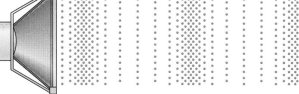

You can see this wave moving if you put a burning candle in front of a loudspeaker. The flame will vibrate backwards and forwards at the same frequency as the loudspeaker.

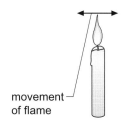

loudspeaker   movement of flame

Sound and a vacuum

If sound reaches you because the air particles transfer it in a wave, that means that it cannot travel if there is nothing to pass it along in a sound wave.

This effect was first shown by a scientist called Francis Hauksbee in 1705, using a clock in a jar. When the air was removed, there was no sound from the clock.

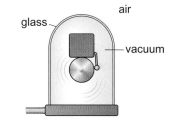

air
glass
vacuum

The diagram shows the same idea using a bell. When all the air has been sucked out of the glass jar, the bell cannot be heard. We say that there is a **vacuum** in the glass jar. This means there are no (or almost no) particles present to pass on the sound. Sound cannot travel through a vacuum because there are no particles to make a sound wave.

Once you leave the Earth's atmosphere, there are no particles to carry sound. You are in the vacuum of space. Astronauts use radio waves to communicate when they are in space. Radio waves are like light – they will travel through a vacuum.

Question 1 | 2

No sound can be heard.

The speed of sound

A simple way to measure the speed of sound is to use a gun that produces a lot of smoke and a very loud sound. The picture shows you how. It is safer if the cannon is loaded with a blank cartridge instead of live shot!

To calculate the speed, you divide the distance the sound travels by the time it takes to get there.

Accurate experiments show that sound travels at 330 m/s in still air. The speed of sound is affected by the wind speed and the amount of water vapour in the air.

The speed of sound is different in different materials. Where particles are closer together, the sound vibrations can be passed along much more quickly. The table gives some typical values.

The speed of high-speed aircraft is often compared with the speed of sound. This is done on a scale called the <u>Mach scale</u>.

When something goes faster than 330 m/s we say it has 'broken the sound barrier'. Speeds above Mach 1 are called <u>supersonic</u>. The first supersonic commercial aircraft was Concorde, which entered service in 1976. It took 3.5 hours to cross the Atlantic from London to New York, cruising for some of the time at Mach 2.

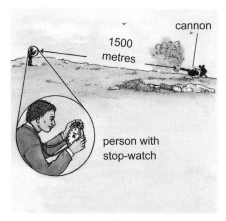

The person with the watch starts it when they see the smoke. They stop the watch when they hear the sound. The watch shows 5 seconds.

Material	Speed of sound in m/s
air	330
water	1500
brick	3000
iron	5000

Mach number	Speed in m/s
Mach 1	330
Mach 2	660
Mach 3	990
Mach 4	41320

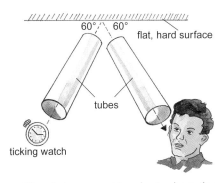

The ticks sound loudest when the tubes are at the same angle to the surface.

Question 3 **4**

Reflections

Sound will reflect off hard surfaces in a similar way to light. You can show this with two tubes and a ticking watch.

Because sound reflects off hard surfaces, things sound different inside concert halls than they do in the open air. Concert halls are designed to produce the sort of sound reflections that performers want and audiences like. These are called **reverberations**. Reverberation is the name for the very faint echoes you hear from different parts of the hall, which reach you at different times.

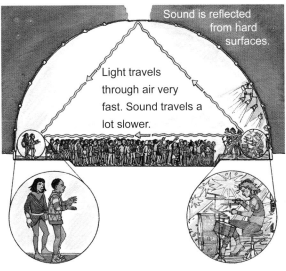

The sound from the drummer reaches the people at the back by different routes.

Question 5

Check your progress

You should already know   Outcomes   Keywords

The ear

The **ear** is the part of the body that converts the vibrations of sound to the messages in nerves that go to the brain.

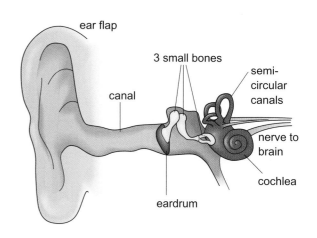

- A sound wave travels down the canal and makes the **eardrum** vibrate.
- These vibrations are passed on to the **cochlea** by a set of three small bones.
- In the cochlea, a liquid moves backwards and forwards, and stimulates the nerve cells inside it.
- The nerve cells make small electrical signals.
- These electrical signals travel along the nerve to the brain.

Question 1

Animals have two ears. This helps the animal to work out the direction that a sound is coming from. This can be useful when catching prey and also when escaping from danger.

Some animals generate sounds that reflect off objects near them. The animal detects the reflected sound and uses the reflection to find its way about. This is how a bat can fly about in the dark and not bump into things. It is called **echolocation**. It is also used by a bat to locate its prey.

Long-eared bat.

Pipistrelle bat.

Bats have large ears to collect faint sounds.

Question 2

Range of hearing

Different animals hear different ranges of sound. The highest note that a human aged about 20 years old can hear has a frequency of about 20 000 Hz. This value drops at about 160 Hz a year from that point on. When humans are about 50 years old, the highest note they can hear is usually about 15 000 Hz.

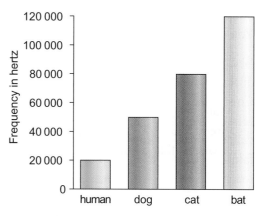

Hearing ranges of different animals.

Dogs, cats and bats can hear much higher notes than humans. Dog owners sometimes use a special whistle that produces a note that is too high for humans to hear, but the dog can hear it. A sound that is higher than the limit of human hearing is called **ultrasonic**. The dog whistle in the photograph produces an ultrasonic sound.

Question 3   4

Damage to hearing

Loud sound waves carry a lot of energy. Very loud sounds can cause you pain in your ears and even do permanent damage. You can get ear pain at a loud rock concert. If you play an MP3 player too loud too often, you can easily damage your hearing.

The loudness of a sound is measured in a unit called the **decibel**. It has the symbol dB. The diagram shows the loudness of some typical sounds. Those higher than 90 dB can cause permanent damage to your hearing if you keep being exposed to them.

Too much noise is called **noise pollution**. People living near airports suffer from noise pollution when aircraft take off and land. There are strict laws to control noise pollution.

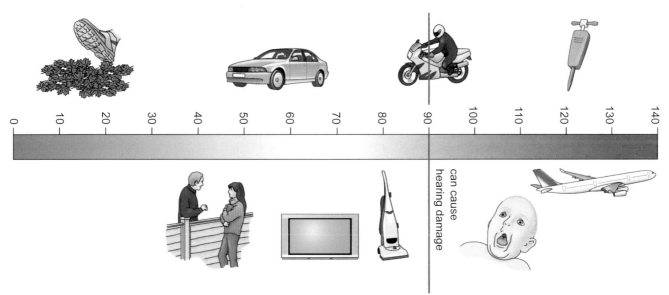

There are also regulations to protect workers who have to do jobs in noisy situations. The worker with the road drill in the photograph is wearing ear protectors, so that the sound that reaches his ears from the drill is not over 90 dB.

Question 5   6

Review your work

Summary ➡

You should already know

Outcomes

Keywords

How good is the experiment?

In science, it is important to be able to decide whether the method you are using is good enough to give you the evidence you are looking for.
We say that you need to **evaluate** the working method. In the experiment that is described below, there are some things that could be improved.

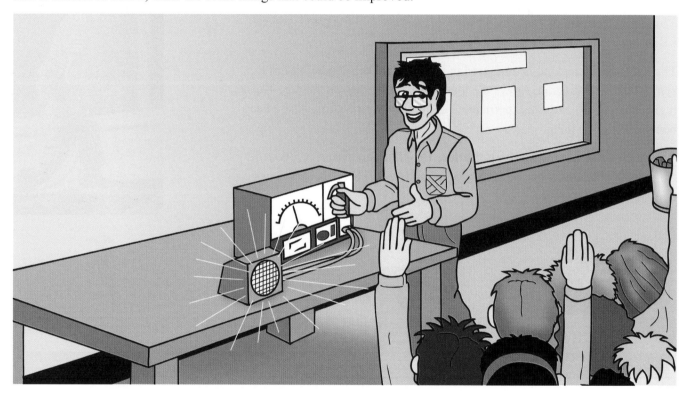

The aim is to find out the highest frequency that pupils can hear.

- The teacher plays a sound.
- The teacher increases the frequency of the sound produced.
- The pupils put up their hands when it becomes too high to hear.

The teacher asks these questions to help pupils evaluate the experiment.

- "Does it matter that you are sitting at different distances from the speaker?"
- "Might you be influenced by when you see others put up their hands?"
- "Not all of you put your hand up at the same time. What is the best way of stating the results of the experiment that takes this into account?"

Question 1 / 2 /

Applying science

Using scientific ideas can help improve people's lives and change the way they live. The high-pitched sounds that are above the human hearing range are called <u>ultrasound</u>. Ultrasound is used to improve people's lives.

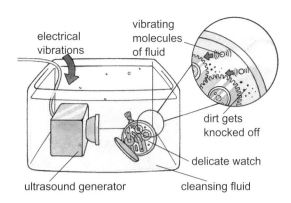

Cleaning things

An ultrasound generator can be used in a small bath of liquid to make ultrasound vibrations throughout the liquid. If you put a delicate piece of machinery like a watch in the liquid then the vibrations of the sound will make the molecules of the liquid knock the dirt off from the machinery.

Dentists use a similar system for cleaning some of the small tools they need to use in your mouth.

Scans

One of the most important uses of ultrasound is to scan someone who is pregnant to look at the fetus before it is born. This is very useful for a doctor to see how the mother and fetus are progressing.

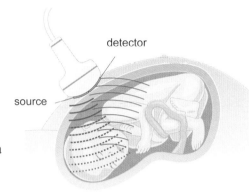

- A probe is moved over the mother's body.
- The probe gives out ultrasound.
- The probe also detects ultrasound that is reflected back from the fetus inside the mother.
- The detected ultrasound is fed into a computer and the software produces a picture on the screen.

This is a good example of the result of **collaboration** between scientists who work in the field of sound and computer software engineers.

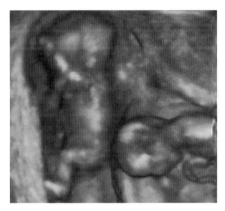

For most people this technique provides a family memento, the first picture for the family album. In some cases, it can give a family an early warning that they are expecting twins, triplets or even more!

Unfortunately, like many applications of science, it can have **moral and ethical issues** associated with it. It is also possible to tell from a scan what gender the fetus is. In some parts of the world, the parents may have a strong opinion about the gender they want their child to have. If the fetus is the 'wrong' gender then they will consider having it aborted.

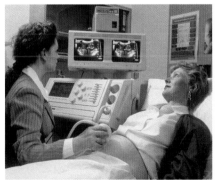

 Question 3 ⟩ **4** ━━━━━━━━━━━━━━━━━━

An ultrasound scan taking place.

8L.1

1 What is sound caused by?

2 Give some different examples of vibrations causing sounds.

3 What can you do to make a sound louder?

4 **a** What is meant by the term <u>amplitude</u>?

   b How does amplitude relate to the loudness of a sound?

5 **a** What is <u>pitch</u>?

   b How does pitch depend upon frequency?

6 The note middle C on the piano has a frequency of 256 Hz.

   a What does 'Hz' stand for?

   b What does <u>256 Hz</u> tell you about the strings that the piano hammer hits when the note is played?

7 How do a microphone and an oscilloscope combine to represent the different aspects of a sound wave?

8L.2

1 How can you show that the vibrations of a loudspeaker produce vibrations in the air in front of it?

2 **a** What is the name for a space from which almost all the particles of gas have been removed so that it is virtually empty?

   b How could you show that sound will not travel across this space?

3 **a** How could you measure the speed of sound?

   b List <u>two</u> of the things which might affect your result.

4 **a** If a jet aeroplane is flying at a speed of 700 m/s, how fast is it going compared with the speed of sound? Give your answer as a Mach number.

   b How could you describe the speed?

5 **a** Why is the sound of someone singing or playing an instrument in the open air different to the sound you get in a concert hall?

   b Suggest why concert halls have many hard, shiny surfaces rather than surfaces draped in soft fabric.

8L.3

1 Describe how your ear detects sound.

2 **a** Why is it useful for animals to have sensitive hearing?

   b Some animals use <u>echolocation</u>.
       Explain what this is.

3 Name <u>two</u> animals that can hear sounds that are above the limit of human hearing.

4 What does the term <u>ultrasonic</u> mean?

5 **a** What is <u>noise pollution</u>?

   b Suggest things that could be done to reduce it.

6 **a** How can loud sounds be dangerous?

   b What can be done to reduce the danger?

8L.HSW

1 Imagine that you are in the class where the experiment is taking place.
   Write out a set of instructions for someone to follow so that they can carry out the experiment. Include a way of displaying the results.

2 Look at the three questions asked by the teacher.

   a Suggest answers to the questions.

   b How good do you think the experiment was?

   c Suggest ways of improving it.

3 Describe <u>two</u> scientific developments in sound that have resulted in improvements in the ways that people live their lives.

4 What moral and ethical issues are associated with ultrasound scans of people who are pregnant?

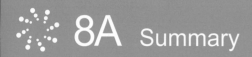

Keywords

To stay healthy we need a balanced diet.

The amount of each food group that we need depends on:

- our age;
- our size;
- our sex;
- how active we are.

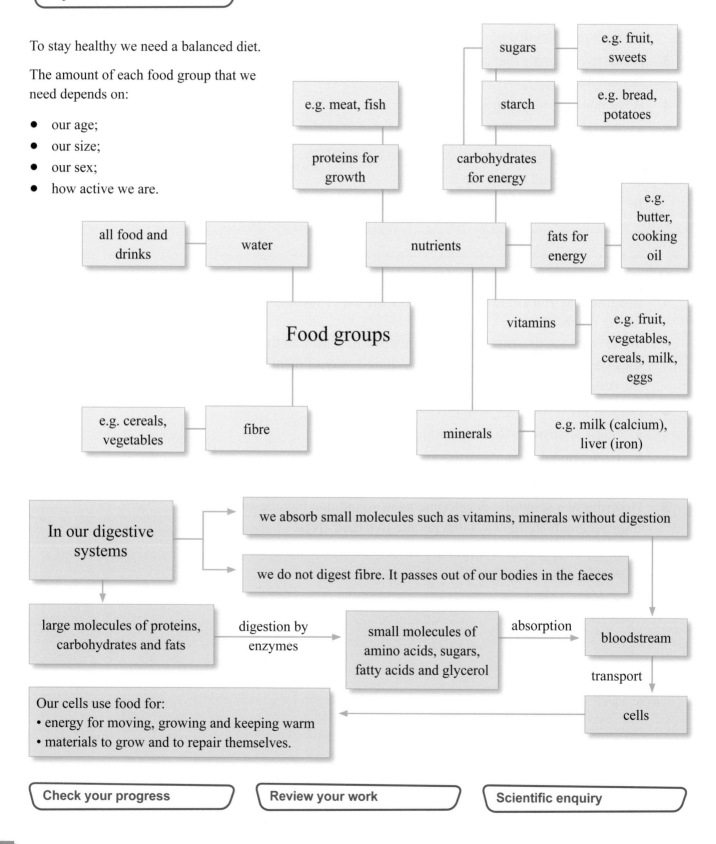

Check your progress

Review your work

Scientific enquiry

Keywords

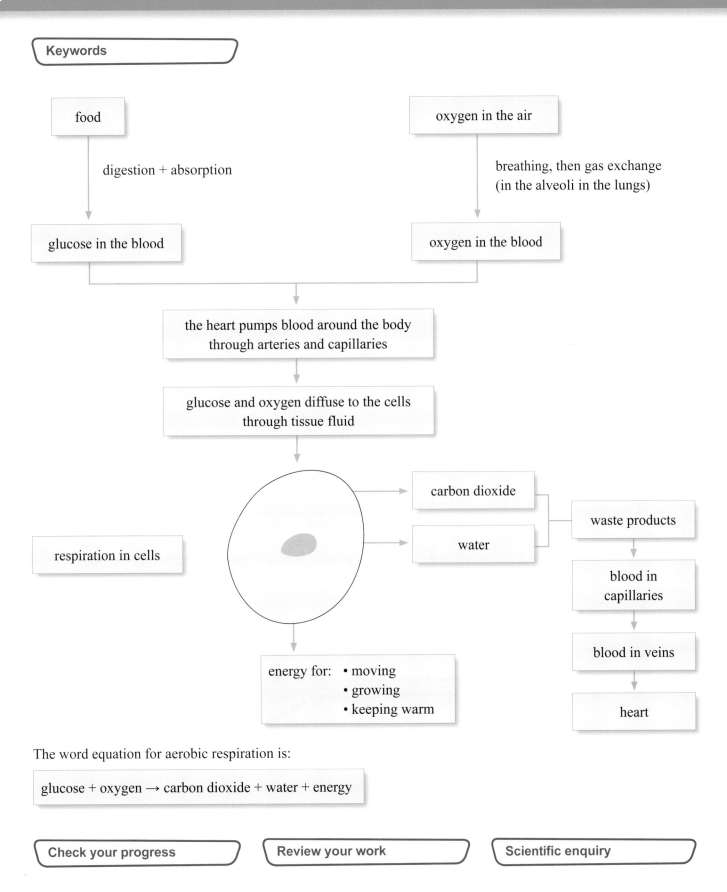

food

digestion + absorption

glucose in the blood

oxygen in the air

breathing, then gas exchange
(in the alveoli in the lungs)

oxygen in the blood

the heart pumps blood around the body
through arteries and capillaries

glucose and oxygen diffuse to the cells
through tissue fluid

respiration in cells

carbon dioxide

water

waste products

blood in
capillaries

blood in veins

heart

energy for: • moving
             • growing
             • keeping warm

The word equation for aerobic respiration is:

glucose + oxygen → carbon dioxide + water + energy

Check your progress   Review your work   Scientific enquiry

Keywords

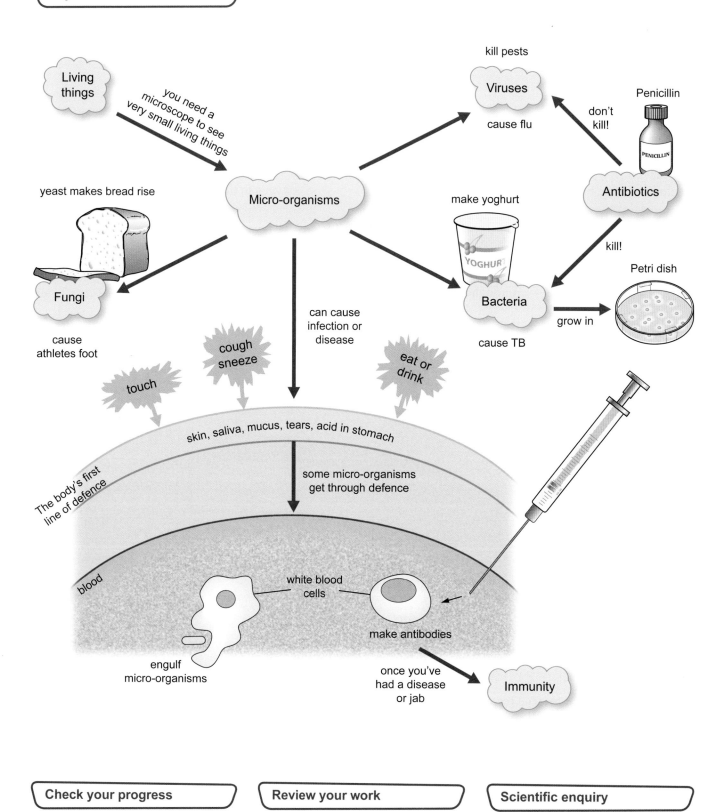

Living things → you need a microscope to see very small living things → **Micro-organisms**

Micro-organisms → **Viruses** — cause flu — kill pests

Penicillin — **Antibiotics** don't kill! → Viruses

yeast makes bread rise — **Fungi** — cause athletes foot

Micro-organisms — can cause infection or disease

make yoghurt — **Bacteria** — cause TB

Antibiotics kill! → **Bacteria** grow in → Petri dish

touch — cough sneeze — eat or drink

skin, saliva, mucus, tears, acid in stomach

The body's first line of defence

some micro-organisms get through defence

blood

white blood cells — engulf micro-organisms

make antibodies

once you've had a disease or jab → **Immunity**

Keywords

Animals with backbones are called vertebrates.

Animals without backbones are called invertebrates.

We classify plants and animals into smaller groups.

Plants are divided into two groups: those with a transport system (vascular) and those without a transport system (non-vascular).

Some factors that affect behaviour are internal (e.g. hormones). Others are external (e.g. tides).

The behaviour of animals affects their survival.

Some behaviour is innate, some is learned.

The place where a plant or animal lives is called its habitat.

Plants and animals have features that suit them to where they live. We say they are adapted to their environmental conditions.

The plants and animals in a habitat interact.

A collection of species living in an area is called a community.

A group of organisms of the same species in an area is called the population.

To find the population size of an organism in an area we can use a quadrat.

An organism that makes its own food is called a producer.

Living things in a community depend on each other.

An animal that only eats plants is called a herbivore.

An animal that cannot make its own food, but gets it from other animals or plants is called a consumer.

An animal that feeds on other animals is called a carnivore.

A number of food chains joined together is called a food web.

Food chains show what animals eat.

A pyramid of numbers is a pyramid shaped diagram showing the numbers of organisms at each stage of a food chain.

Check your progress

Review your work

Scientific enquiry

Key ideas

- An element is a substance that is made from just one type of particle, called an atom.

- There are about 100 elements.

- About 80 of the elements are metals.

- Each element has its own symbol.

- The symbols for elements are universal.

- Elements combine to make different materials.

- Materials are used to make objects.

- Some elements were known in ancient times, but other elements have been discovered more recently.

- Information about elements is collected together in the periodic table.

- There are vertical columns in the periodic table called groups

- Elements in the same group have similar properties.

- Atoms can combine to make molecules.

- We use models to visualise molecules.

- Two or more different elements combine to form a compound.

- A chemical change makes new substances because the atoms join together in different combinations.

- New materials made in a chemical change have different properties from the substances they are made from.

- Chemical changes are different from physical changes.

- A physical change does not change the way atoms are joined to each other.

Check your progress   Review your work   Scientific enquiry

Key ideas

- A compound contains different types of atom joined together.

- The formula of a substance tells us the proportions of each type of atom present in the substance.

- A sample of a compound will always have the same elements present in the same fixed proportions.

- A compound has a chemical name like 'sodium chloride'.

- A chemical formula is used to describe the number of different atoms in one particle of a compound.

- There are different types of reaction, including combustion, neutralisation, precipitation and thermal decomposition.

- Reactions can be described with word equations and with chemical equations

- A chemical equation uses the formulae for the substances taking part in the reaction.

- A mixture is formed when two or more substances are added together but do not react.

- Air is a mixture of gases that can be separated into pure substances.

- Air consists of nitrogen, oxygen, argon (and other noble gases), carbon dioxide and water vapour.

- Each of the gases found in air has important uses.

- Air can be liquefied, and then the individual gases can be separated by fractional distillation.

- Sea water and mineral water are other examples of mixtures.

- Elements and compounds melt and boil at certain temperatures.

- Mixtures do not melt or boil at one particular temperature.

- The melting point and boiling point of a mixture change as the composition of the mixture changes.

Keywords

Key ideas

- Rocks are made of a mixture of mineral grains.

- Non-porous rocks do not let liquids or gases pass through them.

- Porous rocks let liquids and gases pass through them.

- Sedimentary rocks are formed when sediments settle on the bottom of the sea.

- Limestone is an example of a sedimentary rock.

- Weathering breaks down rocks.

- Acid rain causes chemical weathering.

- Physical weathering is caused by changes in temperature.

- When water freezes in cracks, it expands and breaks off bits of rock.

- When the surface of a rock expands and contracts as temperature changes, it can crack.

- Plants and animals can cause weathering – this is called biotic weathering.

- When rocks rub against each other and wear each other away it is called abrasion.

- Weathering can produce rock fragments.

- Rock fragments are moved by gravity, wind and water.

- Rivers carry some rock fragments to the sea.

- Rock fragments are deposited as sediment.

- Hard parts of dead plants and animals can form fossils in sedimentary rock.

- The processes of weathering and the formation of sedimentary rocks happen very slowly.

- We measure the very long times needed for rocks to form on a scale called geological time.

- Scientists who study rocks are called geologists.

Check your progress   Review your work   Scientific enquiry

Key ideas

- Sedimentary rocks can be changed by pressure and high temperature into metamorphic rocks.

- Sedimentary rocks are changed over millions of years as they are buried deeper inside the Earth.

- There is molten rock inside the Earth called magma.

- When magma cools, it solidifies into rock called igneous rock.

- Igneous rocks with large crystals are formed when magma cools slowly.

- Igneous rocks with tiny crystals are formed when magma cools quickly.

- When magma comes out of the Earth's surface, it is called lava.

- When lava comes out on the Earth's surface, it is called an eruption.

- A volcano can be formed from an eruption of lava.

- All types of rock can be broken down by the weather and eventually end up as material in sedimentary rock.

- The constant recycling of material through sedimentary, metamorphic and igneous rocks is called the rock cycle.

Check your progress

Review your work

Scientific enquiry

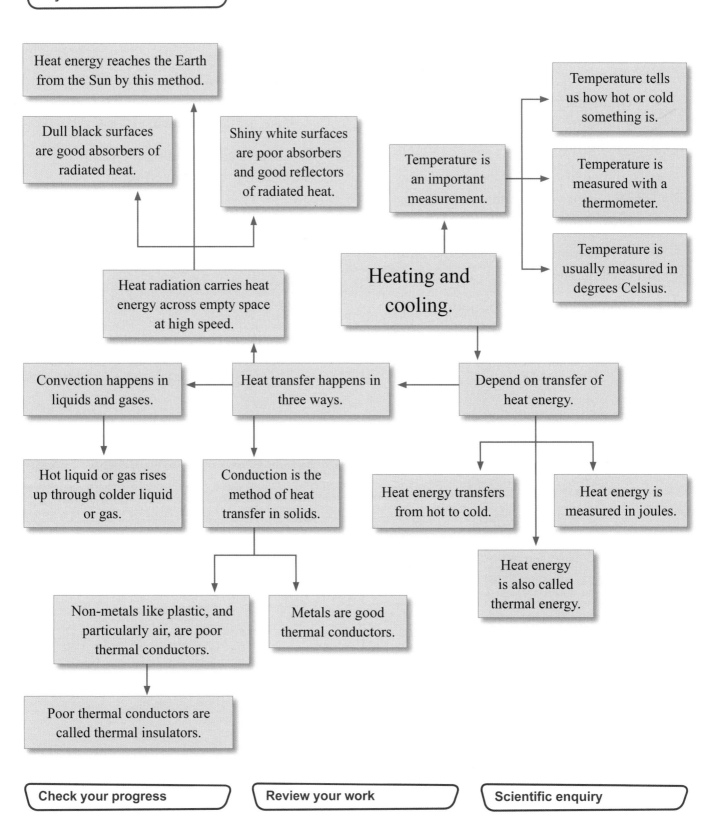

Heat energy reaches the Earth from the Sun by this method.

Dull black surfaces are good absorbers of radiated heat.

Shiny white surfaces are poor absorbers and good reflectors of radiated heat.

Temperature is an important measurement.

Temperature tells us how hot or cold something is.

Temperature is measured with a thermometer.

Temperature is usually measured in degrees Celsius.

Heat radiation carries heat energy across empty space at high speed.

Heating and cooling.

Convection happens in liquids and gases.

Heat transfer happens in three ways.

Depend on transfer of heat energy.

Hot liquid or gas rises up through colder liquid or gas.

Conduction is the method of heat transfer in solids.

Heat energy transfers from hot to cold.

Heat energy is measured in joules.

Heat energy is also called thermal energy.

Non-metals like plastic, and particularly air, are poor thermal conductors.

Metals are good thermal conductors.

Poor thermal conductors are called thermal insulators.

Check your progress   Review your work   Scientific enquiry

Key ideas

- Magnets can attract and repel one another.

- Magnets attract magnetic materials.

- Examples of magnetic materials are iron, cobalt and nickel.

- Non-magnetic materials are not affected by magnets.

- The magnetic force passes through non-magnetic materials.

- The ends of magnets are called poles.

- The south-seeking pole points south and the north-seeking pole points north.

- A north-seeking pole and a south-seeking pole attract each other, but two south-seeking poles or two north-seeking poles repel each other.

- The area around magnets is called a magnetic field.

- Magnetic field lines can be plotted with a compass.

- The direction of the magnetic field goes from the magnet's north pole to its south pole.

- Stronger magnets are represented by showing more lines of force around them.

- The Earth behaves as if it had a giant magnet inside it.

- A compass contains a small magnet that is free to turn.

- The magnet in a compass lines up with the Earth's magnetic field.

- You can make your own magnet by stroking a piece of iron with one end of a magnet.

- When an electric current flows through a wire, there is a magnetic field around the wire.

- Magnets made using electricity are called electromagnets.

- An electromagnet consists of a coil of wire that carries an electric current.

- Electromagnets can be switched on and off.

- You can change the strength of an electromagnet by changing the size of the current, having more turns on the coil or placing a piece of iron called a core inside the coil of wire.

- Relay switches use the current from one circuit to switch on the current in another circuit.

- A relay contains an electromagnet.

Check your progress   Review your work   Scientific enquiry

Keywords

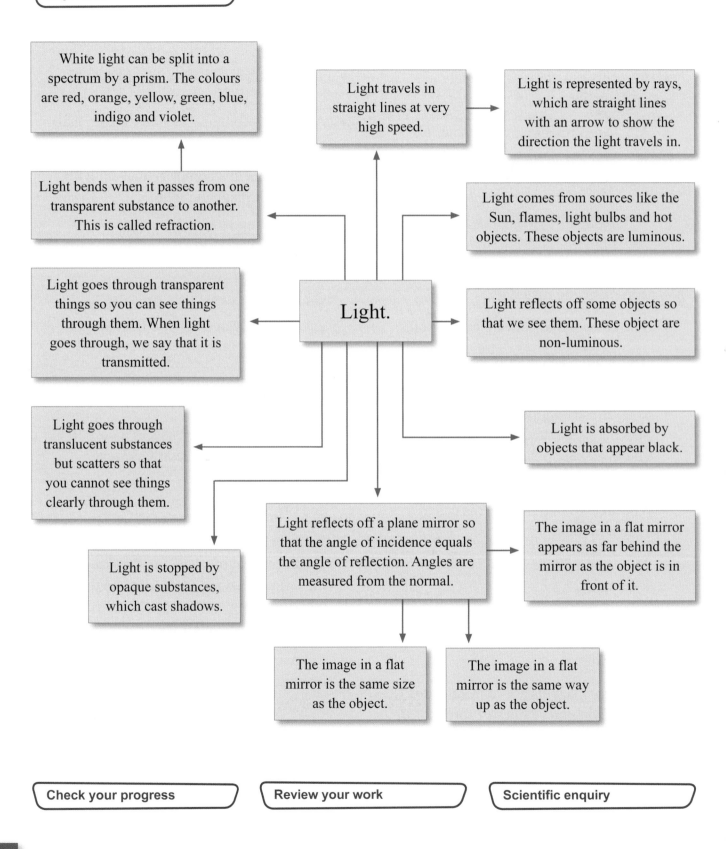

White light can be split into a spectrum by a prism. The colours are red, orange, yellow, green, blue, indigo and violet.

Light travels in straight lines at very high speed.

Light is represented by rays, which are straight lines with an arrow to show the direction the light travels in.

Light bends when it passes from one transparent substance to another. This is called refraction.

Light comes from sources like the Sun, flames, light bulbs and hot objects. These objects are luminous.

Light goes through transparent things so you can see things through them. When light goes through, we say that it is transmitted.

Light.

Light reflects off some objects so that we see them. These object are non-luminous.

Light goes through translucent substances but scatters so that you cannot see things clearly through them.

Light is absorbed by objects that appear black.

Light is stopped by opaque substances, which cast shadows.

Light reflects off a plane mirror so that the angle of incidence equals the angle of reflection. Angles are measured from the normal.

The image in a flat mirror appears as far behind the mirror as the object is in front of it.

The image in a flat mirror is the same size as the object.

The image in a flat mirror is the same way up as the object.

Check your progress

Review your work

Scientific enquiry

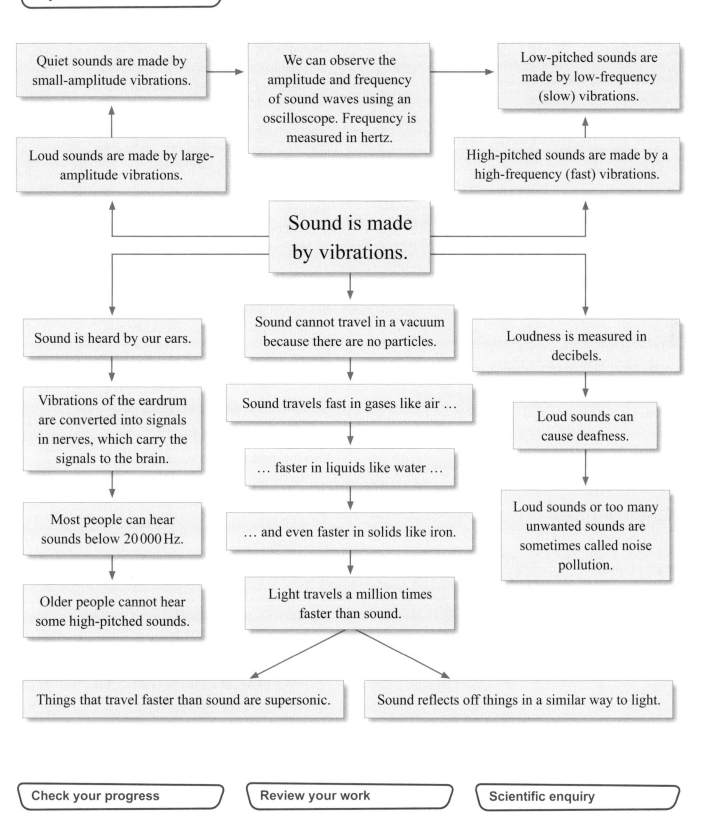

Quiet sounds are made by small-amplitude vibrations.

We can observe the amplitude and frequency of sound waves using an oscilloscope. Frequency is measured in hertz.

Low-pitched sounds are made by low-frequency (slow) vibrations.

Loud sounds are made by large-amplitude vibrations.

High-pitched sounds are made by a high-frequency (fast) vibrations.

Sound is made by vibrations.

Sound is heard by our ears.

Sound cannot travel in a vacuum because there are no particles.

Loudness is measured in decibels.

Vibrations of the eardrum are converted into signals in nerves, which carry the signals to the brain.

Sound travels fast in gases like air …

Loud sounds can cause deafness.

Most people can hear sounds below 20 000 Hz.

… faster in liquids like water …

Older people cannot hear some high-pitched sounds.

… and even faster in solids like iron.

Loud sounds or too many unwanted sounds are sometimes called noise pollution.

Light travels a million times faster than sound.

Things that travel faster than sound are supersonic.

Sound reflects off things in a similar way to light.

Glossary/Index

A

abrasion   wear caused by one substance rubbing against another   100

absorb, absorption   take in a substance; for example living cells take in oxygen and nutrients   9, 10, 12

absorbed (of light)   when light falls onto something and is 'soaked up' by it so that it does not reflect or go through; and object that absorbs all the light that falls onto it will appear dull black   144

aerobic   using oxygen   18, 22

aerobic respiration   using oxygen to break down food to release energy   36

alveoli   tiny round parts that make up the air sacs in the lungs; one is an alveolus   24

amplitude   the distance from the centre position of a wave to the peak; the loudness of sound   156

anaerobic respiration   release of energy from food without the use of oxygen   36

angle of incidence   the angle between an incident ray and the normal   146

angle of reflection   the angle between a reflected ray and the normal   146

antibiotics   drugs used to kill bacteria in the body   42

antibodies   chemicals made by white blood cells to destroy bacteria and other micro-organisms   42

arteries   blood vessels that carry blood away from the heart   20

atmosphere   the mixture of gases that surrounds a planet; on the Earth, the atmosphere is often referred to as 'the air'   86

atoms   the smallest particle of an element   68

attract   two objects pulling towards each other   130

B

bacteria   micro-organisms that are cells without true nuclei; one is called a bacterium   36, 42

bacteriophages   viruses that infect bacteria   44

behaviour patterns   behaviour characteristic of members of a species of animal   52

biased   in the case of an opinion, based on someone's feelings rather than all the facts   60

biotic weathering   the breakdown of rocks caused by plants and animals   98

breathe, breathing   taking air in and out of the lungs   18, 24

breeding behaviour   behaviour associated with breeding, such as courtship, mating or nest building   52

C

capillaries   narrow blood vessels with walls only one cell thick   20

carbohydrates   carbon compounds used by living things as an energy source, for example starch and sugars   2, 4, 8

carbon dioxide   a gas in the air produced by living things in respiration, in combustion or burning and when an acid reacts with a carbonate   18, 28, 30, 86

digestion   the breakdown of large, insoluble molecules into small soluble ones which can be absorbed   9

disease   when some part of a plant or animal isn't working properly   36, 42

E

ear   the organ of hearing   160

eardrum   a tightly stretch skin found at the end of the ear canal; it vibrates when sound reaches it   160

echolocation   a method used to judge the distance to objects, used by bats. This involves sending out a high pitched sound which reflects off objects   160

egest   get rid of faeces from the digestive system   12

electromagnet   a device which becomes magnetic when an electric current flows through a wire coil   134

element   a substance that can't be split into anything simpler by chemical reactions   66, 68

emitter   an object or surface that gives something out for example a hot surface will emit a lot of infra red radiation   124

energy   energy is needed to make things happen   2, 18, 30

environmental conditions   conditions such as light level and temperature in the environment   54

enzymes   protein substances made in cells; they speed up chemical reactions   10

epidemic   an outbreak of a disease affecting a large number of people   40

epidemiology   the study of the causes of disease   26

equation   in chemistry, this is a set of words or symbols that shows what is happening in a chemical reaction   78

erupts   when lava, volcanic ash and gases come out onto the surface of the Earth   110

ethical   an ethical idea is one that relates to a set of moral principles   90

evaluate   to consider how good an experiment or procedure was and how it could be improved   162

evidence   observations and measurements on which theories are based   20, 104

expansion   when a substance gets bigger because its particles speed up and move further apart   98

F

faeces   undigested waste that passes out through the anus   12

fats   part of our food that we use for energy   2, 4, 8

fibre   undigestible cellulose in our food; it prevents constipation   4, 8, 12

food chain   a diagram showing what animals eat   58

food web   a diagram showing what eats what in a habitat   58

formula   uses symbols to show how many atoms of elements are joined together to form a molecule of an element or a compound   78

fossils   remains of plants and animals from long ago   102

fractional distillation   the separation of a mixture of liquids by distillation   84

frequency   the number of waves (for example sound waves) produced every second   156

fungi   a group of living things, including micro-organisms such as moulds and yeasts which cannot make their own food; one is called a fungus   36

G

gas exchange   taking useful gases into a body or cell and getting rid of waste gases   24

geological time   divisions of time based on the ages of rocks   102

periodic table a table of the elements arranged in order so that similar elements are in the same column or group   72

periscope a device made from two mirrors, which can be used to see over walls or from submarines that are under water   146

phages a shortened name for bacteriophages   44

photosynthesis the process by which green plants convert carbon dioxide and water to food using sunlight; oxygen is produced as a result of the process   86

physical change a change that does not involve making any new substances; changes of state, dissolving and being broken in pieces are all types of physical change   70

physical weathering breakdown of rocks by physical processes such as water freezing and expanding in cracks, and by expansion and contraction of the surface as rocks heat up and cool down   98

population all the plants or animals of one species that live in a particular place   54

porous describes the texture of a rock with pores   96

precipitation when a solid is formed in a solution   80

predictions statements about things we think will happen   74

preliminary tests tests, trial runs and information searches carried out to find out the best approach to an investigation   6

pressure how much pushing force there is on an area   108

primary sources original sources of information such as measurements in experiments; as opposed to secondary sources such as information from the Internet   138

prism a device, made of glass or plastic, which refracts light twice, it can be used to produce a spectrum   150

producer a name given to green plants because they produce food   58

properties how something behaves   72

protein nutrient needed for growth and repair; made up of amino acids   2, 8

pyramid of numbers pyramid-shaped diagram that shows how the numbers of living things change along a food chain   58

Q

quadrat an object, often a square frame, used for sampling living things   54, 60

qualitative described using words   138

quantitative described using numbers   138

R

radiation (of heat) a method of heat transfer in which the heat energy is given out as infra-red waves   122

range the difference between the lowest and the highest of a set of readings   104

ray a beam of light that travels in a straight line   142

reflected bounced back, for example light will reflect off a mirror   144

refraction bending of a ray of light when it travels from a material of one density to one of a different density   148

relay a device that uses an electromagnet to switch on one circuit when a second circuit is complete   136

repair mend damaged cells, tissues or organs   2

repel push apart   130

respiration the breakdown of food to release energy in living cells   18, 30, 36

reverberations the repeated echoes of sound caused by reflections off the walls and surfaces in a room   158

risk factors the hazards of an activity or experiment   26

rock cycle the way that the material that rocks are made from is constantly moved around and changed from one type of rock to another 112

rock fragments tiny pieces of rock broken off by physical weathering 100

S

sample collect data about a part of an area or a population to get an idea of the whole 54

scientific papers reports by scientists of their investigations that are published in scientific journals 60

secondary data data from other people's experiments, from books and the Internet 60

secondary sources sources of information such as reports of other people's experiments, books and the Internet 138

sedimentary rocks rocks formed when sediments are compacted and cemented; sandstone and limestone are examples 100

sediments rock fragments that settle on the bed of a river, lake or sea 100

sex hormones hormones associated with reproduction and the reproductive system 52

small intestine the narrow part of the intestine between the stomach and the large intestine; where digestion finishes and absorption happens. 10, 12

south-seeking pole the end of a magnet which is attracted to the Earth's South Pole when allowed to spin freely 130

spectrum white light split into its seven constituent colours, a rainbow is an example of a spectrum 150

surveys in science, ways of investigating habitats, ecosystems, land use, people's opinions etc. 60

sustainable development the idea of improving the quality of life for humans without using up resources that cannot be replaced 86, 88

symbols a shorthand way of writing the names of elements 68

T

technological developments changes in technology which mean that humans can do more things 152

tectonic plates very large pieces of the Earth's crust that move about very slowly 114

temperature a measure of the heat energy contained in hot objects 118

thermal conductors substances that allow thermal energy to pass through them easily by conduction 120

thermal decomposition when a compound is broken down using heat 80

thermal energy the energy something possesses owing to the movement of the particles that it is made of; sometimes referred to as 'heat energy' 120

thermal insulators substances that do not let thermal energy pass through them easily by conduction 120

thermal radiation another name for infra-red radiation; this is given out by a substance because of its temperature 122

thermometer a device used to measure temperature 118

tissue fluid liquid between all the cells of your body through which dissolved substances diffuse 18

translucent allows light to pass through but breaks it up so that there is no clear image 144

transmitted allows something to pass through 144

Alamy 8B.HSW.a (Blain Harrington III), 8D.2.b (David Hosking), 8E.2.a (Andrew Palmer), 8F.4.d (Phototake Inc.), 8K.HSW.a (Jupiterimages/Stock images); **Andrew Lambert** 8E.3.b, 8E.3c, 8E.4.a, 8F.4.b, 8F.5.b, 8G.1.a, 8G.1.b, 8G.1.c, 8G.1.d, 8G.1.e, 8G.1.f, 8G.1.g, 8G.2.b, 8G.2.c, 8G.2.d, 8G.4.d, 8G.HSW.a, 8L.1.b; **Cambridge University Press** 8G.4.a (Joanne Robinson); **Chris Westwood** 8G.3.c; **Corbis** 8B.3.a (Moonboard), 8B.3.b (Roger Ressmeyer), 8G.3.d (Michael Busselle), 8G.4.b (Chinch Gryniewicz/Ecoscene), 8H.1.h (Charles O'Rear), 8H.2.f (Yann Arthus-Betrand); **Ecoscene** 8D.3.a, 8D.3.b, 8D.3.d (Chinch Gryniewicz), 8D.3.h, 8D.3.k (Sally Morgan), 8D.3.j (Kevin King), 8F.6.b (Paul Thompson), 8F.HSW.c (Jim Winkley), 8F.HSW.e (Susan Cunningham); **education.co.uk/ walmsley** 8L.1.c, 8L.3.c; **Fisher Scientific** 8I.HSW.a; **Geoscience Features Picture Library** 8F.2.c, 8F.5.a, 8G.2.f, 8H.1.a, 8H.1.b, 8H.1.c, 8H.1.e, 8H.1.f, 8H.1.g, 8H.2.b (Dr B.Booth), 8G.4.e (D. Bayliss), 8H.2.a (M. Hobbs), 8H.2.e (University of California); **Graham Burns** 8D.4.b; **Istituto e Museo di Storia della Scienza Florence** 8I.1.c; **Jean Martin** 8D.3.c, 8D.3.e, 8D.3.f; **Life File** 8F.6.a (Christopher Jones); **Mary Evans Picture Library** 8A.5.a; **Mediscan** 8A.5.c; **Nature Picture Library** 8L.3.a (Artur Tabor); **NHPA** 8D.HSW.a (Manfred Danegger), 8D.HSW.b (Roger Tidman), 8G.4.c (Daniel Heudin); **PA Photos** 8I.4.a (Phil Nobel/PA Archive); **Panos Pictures** 8F.HSW.d (Erik Schaffer); **Photolibrary** 8A.3.a, 8A.3.c (Martin Brigdale), 8A.3.b (Eaglemoss Consumer Publications); **Professional Sport** 8B.1.b, 8B.5.c (Tommy Hindley); **Redferns Music Picture Library** 8L.1.a; **Robert Harding Picture Library Ltd** 8F.3.b (S. Frieberg), 8G.2.e (John Start); **Science Photo Library** 8A.1.b (Peter Menzel), 8A.1.c, 8A.1.d (Biophoto Associated), 8A.5.b (Alain Pol, ISM), 8B.1.a (Cristina Pedrazzini), 8B.1.c (Jeremy Walker), 8B.2.a (Sheila Terry), 8B.2.b (Alfred Pasieka), 8B.3.c (James King-Holmes), 8B.4.a (Alfred Pasieka) 8C.1.a (R. Maisonneuve, Publiphoto Diffusion), 8C.2.a (Jane Shemitt), 8C.4.a (Noble Proctor), 8C.HSW.a (Louise Murray), 8C.HSW.b (Volker Steger), 8D.1.a (Dr. Jeremy Burgess), 8D.3.g (John Heseltine), 8D.2.a (Vanessa Vick), 8D.2.c (Duncan Shaw), 8D.2.d, 8D.4.a (Lepus), 8E.1.b (Pascal Goetgheluck), 8E.1.c 9Claude Nuridsany & Marie Perennou), 8E.2.b (Susumu Nishinaga), 8E.3.d (Jerry Mason), 8E.HSW.a, 8F.1.a (Alfred Pasieka), 8F.1.b (Andrew McClenaghan), 8F.2.a (Martyn F. Chillmaid), 8F.2.b (Charles D. Winters), 8F.3.a (Sheila Terry), 8F.4.a (Tony McConnell), 8F.4.c (David Taylor), 8F.HSW.a (J.C. Revy), 8F.HSW.b (Biophoto Associates), 8F.HSW.f (Martin Bond), 8G.2.g (Tony Craddock), 8G.3.e (John Mead), 8H.1.d (George Bernard), 8H.1.i (G. Brad Lewis), 8H.1.j (Martin Bond), 8H.2.c (Oscar Burriel), 8H.2.d (Soames Summerhays), 8I.1.a (Astrid & Hans Frieder Michler), 8I.1.b (Chris Priest & Mark Clarke), 8K.HSW.b (R. Maisonneuve, Publiphoto Diffusion), 8L.HSW.a (Dr Najeeb Layyous), 8L.HSW.b (Saturn Stills); **The Allan Cash Picture Library** 8E.3.a; **Vanessa Miles** 8B.5.a, 8B.5.b, 8D.3.i, 8E.1.a, 8G.2.a, 8G.3.b, 8J.1.a, 8L.3.b; **Wellcome Photo Library** 8A.1.a (Fiona Progoff), 8A.2.a; **Wilderness Photographic Library** 8G.3.a.

Image references show the Unit and Topic of the book (eg. 8A.1) and the order of the image in the Topic from top to bottom, left to right (e.g. 8A.1.b is the second photograph in Topic 1 of Unit 8A).

Series advisors Andy Cooke, Jean Martin
Series authors Sam Ellis, Jean Martin

Series consultants Diane Fellowes-Freeman, Richard Needham

Based on original material by Derek Baron, Trevor Bavage, Paul Butler, Andy Cooke, Zoe Crompton, Sam Ellis, Kevin Frobisher, Jean Martin, Mick Mulligan, Chris Ram